Knowledge-based | Skills-orientated | Experiences-infused

POWER UP Your Curriculum

AF822167

A PRACTICAL HANDBOOK FOR TEACHERS, TEAMS, SCHOOLS AND PARENTS

Bruce Robertson

hachette LEARNING

hachette LEARNING

Together we unlock every learner's unique potential

At Hachette Learning (formerly Hodder Education), there's one thing we're certain about. No two students learn the same way. That's why our approach to teaching begins by recognising the needs of individuals first.

Our mission is to allow every learner to fulfil their unique potential by empowering those who teach them. From our expert teaching and learning resources to our digital educational tools that make learning easier and more accessible for all, we provide solutions designed to maximise the impact of learning for every teacher, parent and student.

Aligned to our parent company, Hachette Livre, founded in 1826, we pride ourselves on being a learning solutions provider with a global footprint.

www.hachettelearning.com

Although every effort has been made to ensure that website addresses are correct at time of going to press, Hachette Learning cannot be held responsible for the content of any website mentioned in this book. It is sometimes possible to find a relocated web page by typing in the address of the home page for a website in the URL window of your browser.

Hachette UK's policy is to use papers that are natural, renewable and recyclable products and made from wood grown in well-managed forests and other controlled sources. The logging and manufacturing processes are expected to conform to the environmental regulations of the country of origin.

To order, please visit www.HachetteLearning.com or contact Customer Service at education@hachette.co.uk / +44 (0)1235 827827.

ISBN: 978 1 0360 2176 4

© Bruce Robertson 2026

First published in 2026 by
Hachette Learning (a trading division of Hodder & Stoughton Limited),
An Hachette UK Company
Carmelite House
50 Victoria Embankment
London EC4Y 0DZ

www.HachetteLearning.com

The authorised representative in the EEA is Hachette Ireland, 8 Castlecourt Centre, Dublin 15, D15 XTP3, Ireland (email: info@hbgi.ie)

Impression number 10 9 8 7 6 5 4 3 2 1
Year 2030 2029 2028 2027 2026

All rights reserved. Apart from any use permitted under UK copyright law, no part of this publication may be reproduced or transmitted in any form or by any means, electronic or mechanical, including photocopying and recording, or held within any information storage and retrieval system, without permission in writing from the publisher or under licence from the Copyright Licensing Agency Limited. Further details of such licences (for reprographic reproduction) may be obtained from the Copyright Licensing Agency Limited, www.cla.co.uk

Illustrations by DC Graphic Design Limited
Typeset in the UK by DC Graphic Design Limited.
Printed in the UK.

A catalogue record for this title is available from the British Library.

FSC www.fsc.org
MIX
Paper | Supporting responsible forestry
FSC™ C104740

'It is a slightly arresting notion that if you were to pick yourself apart with tweezers, one atom at a time, you would produce a mound of fine atomic dust, none of which had ever been alive but all of which had once been you.'

Bill Bryson, *A Short History of Nearly Everything 2.0*

For Ruben, Imogen and Ellis

About the author

Bruce Robertson is the CEO of Next Level Educational, specialising in high-quality professional development for teachers, leaders and schools. His best-selling books include *The Teaching Delusion* trilogy, *Power Up Your Pedagogy* and *Power Up Your Questioning*.

As a headteacher, Bruce's leadership of Berwickshire High School from 2020–24 was instrumental in turning around a school rated 'weak' and 'unsatisfactory' in a national inspection, to one widely recognised as sector-leading in its approaches to teaching and learning improvement, and staff professional development.

As an international professional development consultant and trainer, Bruce's areas of specialism include pedagogy, curriculum, assessment, behaviour and leadership at middle and senior levels. He is widely praised for his passion, clarity and the practicality of his messages.

Testimonials

When schools get the curriculum right, everything else follows. Bruce Robertson's *Power Up Your Curriculum* shows us exactly what "right" looks like. Skills are knowledge in action. Experiences deepen and enrich that knowledge. And meta-skills are best developed not by teaching them directly, but by building the subject knowledge that makes them possible. If your school is embarking on a curriculum review, read this first!

Daisy Christodoulou, Director of Education at No More Marking; author of *Teachers vs Tech, Making Good Progress* and *Seven Myths about Education*

Power Up Your Curriculum establishes afresh the means by which effective curricular design really happens. Among a host of other nuggets, Robertson reminds us about the primacy of knowledge, and how the clarity with which we organize content shapes the precision with which we teach it. This fantastic guide should be required reading for teachers and curriculum designers alike.

Jim Heal, Co-Founder, Learning Science Partners

In *Power Up Your Curriculum*, Bruce Robertson has taken the complexity of curriculum thinking and made it clear, practical and usable. It is grounded in strong principles, but it never loses sight of the realities of schools and classrooms. What is particularly welcome is the emphasis on curriculum as the 'what' of teaching: the knowledge, skills and experiences we want young people to encounter, understand and remember. The distinction between being busy and learning is especially powerful, and will resonate with teachers and leaders alike.

This is a generous, thoughtful and highly practical book. It will support schools to ask better questions, sharpen their curriculum thinking and keep the main thing the main thing: what pupils are learning, why it matters and how we make that learning stronger.

Mary Myatt, education writer and speaker; author of *KS3:The Ambitious Years*

This is another superb book from Bruce, and as we've come to expect from him, it's clear, practical, and informed by the latest evidence from education research. The section on meta-skills is fantastic, as Bruce breaks down the misconceptions around transferable skills and demonstrates the pivotal importance of knowledge. It's that combination of professional experience, willingness to challenge orthodoxy, and clarity of writing that makes him such a compelling voice in global education.

Robin Macpherson, Head of College at Robert Gordon's College; co-author of *What Does This Look Like in the Classroom?* and *The Teaching Life*

We need more Bruce Robertsons in the system. He has that rare ability to take something familiar and make you see it differently. His work on curriculum cuts through the noise and gets to what actually matters: clarity, precision, and purpose. This isn't theory for theory's sake. It's practical, usable, and grounded in what teachers really face day to day. What stands out most is the discipline behind it. There's a rigour to Bruce's thinking that sharpens your own. A teacher that reads this book and applies it consistently, will see the impact of what they do leap forward. A leader that trains their teachers in this will see that happen at scale.

Tom Bennett, OBE, founder of researchED

Power Up Your Curriculum by Bruce Robertson provides a superb roadmap for school leaders and teachers seeking to move beyond superficial curriculum models towards deep, content-rich approaches that will benefit all students. The book includes practical frameworks to help leaders analyse curriculum provision and offers clear steps to implement significant improvements. Drawing on findings from cognitive science, *Power Up Your Curriculum* will be an important catalyst for curriculum change in both primary and secondary schools.

Andrew Percival, Deputy Headteacher at Stanley Road Primary School, Oldham, UK

Contents

Foreword

In 2006, two psychologists, Henry Roediger and Jeffrey Karpicke, published a paper with the unassuming title 'Test-Enhanced Learning'. Its finding was simple but would have far-reaching consequences: that testing yourself on something is not merely a way of measuring what you have learned, but one of the most powerful ways of learning it in the first place. The paper launched a thousand classroom quizzes. Yet what Roediger and Karpicke had really done was to reawaken a line of inquiry begun more than a century earlier, by a solitary German with a peculiar appetite for tedium.

His name was Hermann Ebbinghaus, and in the 1880s he conducted one of the strangest experiments in the history of psychology, using the only subject he entirely trusted: himself. In order to study memory in its purest form, uncontaminated by prior knowledge or association, he invented the nonsense syllable, and set about committing thousands of meaningless consonant–vowel–consonant trigrams (*WID*, *ZOF*, and their many joyless cousins) to memory, testing his own recall at intervals over hours, days and weeks. Out of this peculiar series of experiments came the forgetting curve: the now-familiar demonstration that memory decays sharply and predictably unless something is done to arrest it.

Over 100 years later, the mechanisms for how to operationalise this in a classroom are still not fully understood. A decade ago, you could walk into almost any staffroom in England and say the words 'retrieval practice' to a row of politely blank faces. Today you would be hard pressed to find a teacher who has not heard the term, deployed it or sat through an inset day devoted to it. It has its starters and its knowledge organisers, its low-stakes quizzes and its exit tickets. The passage from obscure laboratory effect to national orthodoxy has been, by the geological standards of educational change, remarkably swift.

This is a success story but success of this kind carries its own pathology. Edward Haertel warns of the *lethal mutation*: the way a good idea, as it spreads, is so often stripped of the very thing that made it work, until only the ritual survives, performed with great diligence and no memory of why. Retrieval practice is now well into its mutating phase, and the mutation exposes a deeper confusion about where the power of good teaching actually lies.

Education has always been prone to what I call the *activity fallacy*: our habit of mistaking the means of learning for its mechanism. The quiz, the starter, the mini-whiteboard, the do-now – these are activities, observable and reassuringly busy. But no activity teaches anything of itself. It works, when it works, only because it compels a particular kind of cognitive effort: the effortful act of retrieval, of thinking hard about something worth thinking about. The activity is the visible shell; the mechanism is the invisible thinking within it. In our zeal to codify the *how* of teaching, we have fallen in love with the shell. We audit whether the retrieval starter happened; we seldom ask whether it made anyone think, or about what.

Which brings us to the thing the activity fallacy conspires to hide. You cannot retrieve what was never taught. You cannot space, interleave or quiz your way to knowledge that was never coherently sequenced in the first place. A quiz is only ever as good as the curriculum it interrogates; strip that curriculum of structure and coherence and even the most impeccable retrieval routine is merely testing children on a jumble of disconnected facts, mistaking motion for progress. The secret lever of good instruction, in other words, is not the technique, it is what the technique serves. It was always the curriculum – the rich, well-built, carefully ordered body of content that alone gives the technique something worth doing.

This is the ground Bruce Robertson stakes out, and it is an often under-examined area of the evidence-informed movement. We spent a decade getting the *how* of teaching right, and we were right to. But pedagogy was always parasitic on content: a brilliant method in service of a threadbare curriculum is a fast car with nowhere to go. The overdue argument of this book is that *what* we teach deserves the same rigour we have lately, and rightly, lavished on how we teach it.

The knowledge-versus-skills debate was always a category error: a quarrel largely between people who could not agree on what either word meant. Robertson's reframing, that skills are simply knowledge in action, dissolves the antagonism rather than declaring a victor, and returns a great deal of wasted energy to the only question that matters: what, precisely, do we want children to know and be able to do, and in what order?

There is, too, a moral seriousness here that is easy to miss beneath the practical scaffolding. A coherent, knowledge-rich curriculum is not merely an efficiency; it is an instrument of equity. The child from the advantaged home arrives already steeped in the background knowledge that makes new learning adhere – the Matthew effect runs in their favour from the very start. The vague, specification-light curriculum, for all its progressive intentions, quietly entrenches that advantage, because it leaves to chance and to home what it ought to guarantee in school. To specify what every child will be taught, clearly and ambitiously, is among the most redistributive acts a school can perform.

What makes Robertson the right guide is that he has done this work, not merely theorised it. Plenty of books will tell you that curriculum matters; rather fewer will show you, concretely, how to build one, specifically through his levels of organisation, his Programmes of Teaching and Learning, the disciplined conversations of his 5Cs. This book crosses the theory-practice gap that swallows so much educational writing, and it does so without condescension and without jargon. Read it as the companion volume to everything we have come to understand about how learning happens: the case, made plainly and usefully, that the *what* of teaching has waited long enough for its turn.

Carl Hendrick, June 2026

Introduction:
Do we really need schools?

Do we really need schools?

Let's kick off with a big question: **Do we really need schools?**

Most people would say yes, and I would agree. But why? What is the purpose of schools?

The purpose of schools

To my mind, Lucy Crehan, author of the wonderful *Cleverlands*, captures the essence of schools beautifully as she considers those she would want for her own children:

> I'd like my children to be excellent readers and solid mathematicians… I want them to have a good understanding of science too… I'd also want them to have a broader education. They may not be good at art or dance if talent has anything to do with genetics, but I'd like them to throw themselves into the creative arts, and learn to express themselves through these mediums. I'd like them to come home from school covered in mud from a rugby game, or stinking of BO after their basketball match… I'd also like their school to encourage them to think about their community, their society and their role within it, and for them to be held to high standards of moral conduct. None of these things are ruled out by sending them to a school [that achieves strong exam results].[1]

My own view is that, first and foremost, the purpose of school is to teach all students to read and write. Schools should also help all students to become proficient at maths, at least to a minimum standard, and ensure all students have the opportunity to develop expertise in this area as they go through school, if they wish to. The same principles should apply to a broad range of subjects, including science, history, geography, music, art and literature. Through learning in subjects, schools should focus on developing students' 'cultural capital',[2] empowering them to understand, appreciate and contribute to the world in

---

1 Crehan, L. (2016) *Cleverlands*

2 Reid, A. (2020) 'Cultural Capital, Critical Theory and Curriculum'

the fullest sense. In short, schools should aim to broaden horizons and open minds, interesting students in subjects and topics they are unlikely to have been interested in had they not gone to school.

Helping students achieve success in exams is also an important purpose of school because qualifications open doors, but exam success shouldn't be seen as more important than learning in the widest sense. With that in mind, for me, a key purpose of school is to give students access to a wide variety of learning opportunities, including sports, clubs, plays and trips. As well as being fun and memorable – both valuable outcomes in their own right – such opportunities can help shape students' character through the development of attributes such as confidence, resilience, humility, self-awareness and kindness, all of which can make students better people than they might otherwise have been had they not gone to school.

In a nutshell then, for me, the purpose of school is to help young people become 'good people' who know and can do a lot, setting them up to live a life fuelled and enriched by the learning that has come as a result of school. To achieve this, we need an excellent curriculum taught by excellent teachers.

The aim and structure of this book

If at least some of this resonates, or if you are interested in exploring these themes further, this is a book for you. At its heart, *Power Up Your Curriculum* is a book about the purpose of school and how we can ensure every student has the opportunity to go to a really great school. It has been written for teachers, leaders, parents and anyone interested in the theme of curriculum generally.

The book is split into two parts:

- **Part 1: Launchpad**
- **Part 2: Curriculum Concepts.**

In **Part 1**, we shall explore three 'launchpad' questions: **(1)** What do we mean by 'curriculum'? **(2)** How good is your curriculum? **(3)** Who should create the curriculum?

This sets up **Part 2**, which builds on the themes discussed to explore six 'Curriculum Concepts':

- **Curriculum Concept 1**: Skills are knowledge in action
- **Curriculum Concept 2**: Knowledge is the catalyst to understanding and future learning
- **Curriculum Concept 3**: The more specific a skill, the more likely it can be taught directly, and the more likely it can be transferred
- **Curriculum Concept 4**: The best way to teach meta-skills is to focus on knowledge
- **Curriculum Concept 5**: When developing your curriculum, start with the big picture and work your way in
- **Curriculum Concept 6**: Power up your curriculum using 5Cs

Real school impact

As headteacher of Berwickshire High School in Scotland, these were the concepts that guided our curriculum improvement focus and which, ultimately, played a key role in transforming experiences and outcomes for students. For example, when we initiated the process of curriculum reform in August 2020, our school was ranked 194th (out of 340 schools) in *The Times Scottish Secondary League Tables*; in the March 2026 rankings, the school was ranked 78th, an increase of 116 places.

All schools can achieve similar transformations. To be successful, 'curriculum' should be high on the list of improvement priorities. *Power Up Your Curriculum* is designed to support every school with that, highlighting concepts, pitfalls and practical approaches to keep everyone on the right track.

Let's get going.

Bruce Robertson, July 2026

Part 1: Launchpad

What do we mean by 'curriculum'?

How good is your curriculum?

Who should create the curriculum?

What do we mean by 'curriculum'?

Let's start with a key question: **What does the word *curriculum* mean to you?**

'The what'

Like many things in education, 'curriculum' is an area we can overcomplicate unnecessarily. **As simple as possible (but not simpler)** is usually a good guiding principle and one we will use throughout this book.[3] Simplicity and user-friendly typically go hand-in-hand.

Accepting this, I would suggest the simplest – and most user-friendly – way to think of the curriculum is as the **what** of teaching (pedagogy is the 'how'). By 'what', we mean the **knowledge and skills** we want students to learn and the **experiences** we want them to have.[4] The catch-all term for these three is **content**.

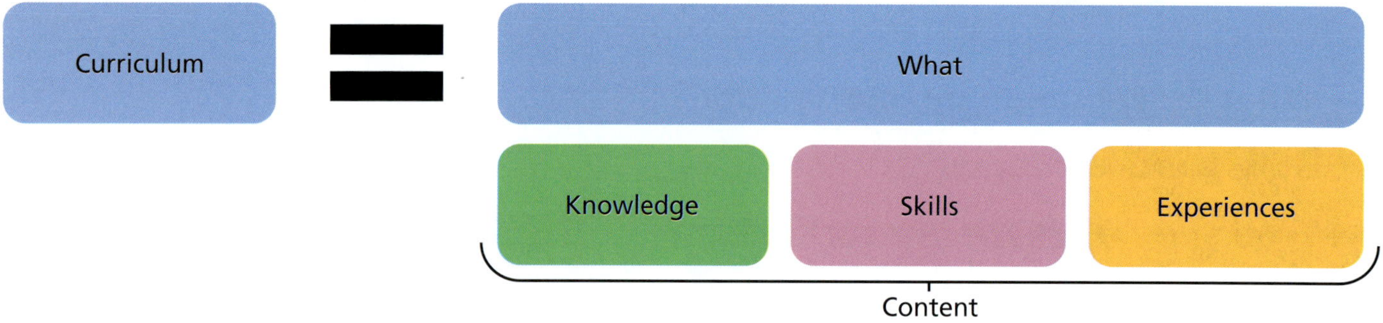

3 This quotation is often attributed to Albert Einstein.

4 Note: When we talk about *experiences*, we don't mean 'pedagogy' (though there can sometimes be overlap between the two). By *experiences*, we mean 'enriching learning opportunities', such as: in drama, watching a live performance of a play; in science, watching a demonstration of the howling jelly-baby experiment; in music, listening to a recording of Beethoven's fifth symphony. Experiences complement pedagogy and develop learning in ways that no other approach could.

What about 'attributes'?

Alongside knowledge, skills and experiences, there is an argument for including 'attributes', by which we mean *behavioural characteristics* or *dispositions*. However, like 'emotions' (such as enjoyment and happiness) or 'success', I would argue that attributes are best thought of separately. Attributes develop **as** knowledge and skills are being learned, and **as** experiences are being had.[5] Like emotions or success, they are **indirect outcomes** of students' engagement with content. Because schools can't plan for the development of attributes in the same, direct way they can knowledge, skills and experiences, 'attributes' should be thought of differently. The way content is taught (pedagogy) often has more of an influence on the development of attributes than the content itself (curriculum).

For example, a student **might** develop confidence (an attribute) as they are solving algebraic equations in maths, depending on how the teacher is teaching this. Crucial to the development of confidence is the experience of success,[6] so whether or not this student develops confidence in solving algebraic equations will depend on the extent to which they are successful.[7] A student **might** develop resilience (a different attribute) through the experience of playing hockey in the school team. Again, whether or not this attribute develops will be heavily influenced by pedagogy, such as the feedback they get from their teacher or coach.

As I made clear in the introduction to this book: schools **do** have a key role to play in the development of attributes. The point being made here is that **attributes develop as students engage with the curriculum** - they aren't the curriculum itself.

---

5 Sherrington, T. (2017) *The Learning Rainforest*

6 Kirschner, P.A. and Hendrick, C. (2020) *How Learning Happens*

7 And of course, just because they develop confidence in solving algebraic equations, it doesn't mean they will be confident in solving other types of problems, or in other subject areas or scenarios. Confidence, like all attributes, is intrinsically linked to the situation at hand.

A good analogy is watching a film. The visuals and audio in the film are 'content', which everyone involved in making the film can control. The reaction an audience has to the film can't be controlled by those who made it – reactions are an indirect outcome of the audience's engagement with content. And so it is with attributes.

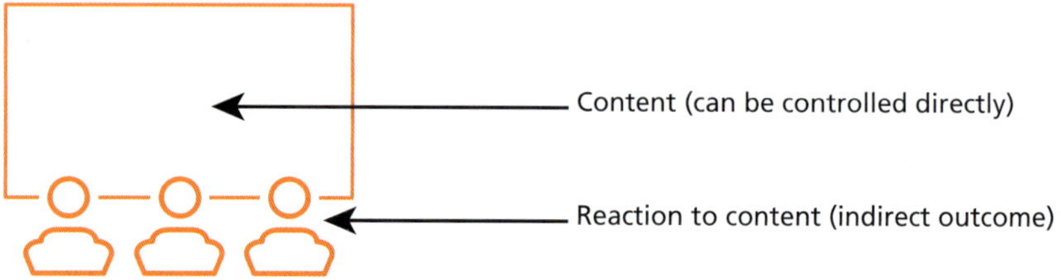

Isn't this just the syllabus?

Some people might argue that the 'what' (content) is just the 'syllabus' and that 'curriculum' should mean more than this. However, I'm not really sure what more we need.

If the answer is **subjects** and **out-of-subject opportunities** (such as sports and clubs), I would suggest these are best thought of as **content organisers**. English is a content organiser for the knowledge, skills and experiences relating to this subject (such as spelling, grammar and literature). The same principle applies to maths, science, history, art, and so on. It also applies to sports, clubs and other out-of-subject opportunities.

Content organiser: English	Content organiser: maths	Content organiser: science club
• Knowledge • Skills • Experiences	• Knowledge • Skills • Experiences	• Knowledge • Skills • Experiences

If the answer is 'resources' (such as textbooks, lesson plans and teachers' guides) or 'approaches to teaching and learning' (such as reading, writing and discussion), we have moved into the territory of pedagogy – **how** content is taught. While there will often be overlap between the 'what' and the 'how', they aren't the same thing. As Dylan Wiliam points out:

> A collection of teaching resources is no more a curriculum than a pile of bricks is a house.[8]

Let's take a moment to explore this in a bit more detail.

Curriculum, pedagogy and assessment

The relationship between curriculum, pedagogy and assessment can be thought of as in the following diagram:[9]

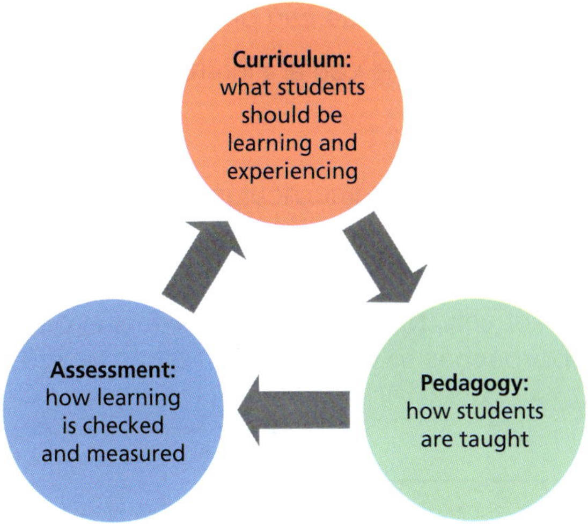

Pedagogy

The same curriculum can be taught in a wide variety of ways. For example, students might be taught about the Vikings – the **curriculum** – via an interactive teacher presentation, through reading, watching a video or researching this topic online – all of which are **pedagogy**. However, just because something can be taught in a wide variety of ways, it doesn't mean all of these will be equally effective. While most pedagogical approaches will work to some extent, not every approach is likely to work equally well all of the time.[10]

---

8 Wiliam, D. (2018) *Creating the Schools Our Children Need*
9 Adapted from Kirschner, P.A., Hendrick, C. and Heal, J. (2022) *How Teaching Happens*
10 Hattie, J. (2012) *Visible Learning for Teachers*

In general, the best pedagogies to use depend on **where students are in their learning**.[11] For anyone who is a relative 'novice' and in the early stages of learning something new (regardless of age), teacher-led approaches are typically the most effective and efficient.[12] This doesn't mean lecturing. Rather, it means teaching that is direct and interactive, with lots of modelling, scaffolding, questioning, discussion, practice and feedback.[13] Such approaches can be thought of as **Specific Teaching**.[14]

As learning develops and students become more 'expert' in a particular area, they are in a stronger position to take more responsibility for their learning and to lead this more themselves. At this stage, less structured approaches, such as through choices and open-ended application, generally become more appropriate. These can be thought of as **Non-Specific Teaching**.[15]

If this is a theme you are interested in exploring further, see Appendix 1: An overview of pedagogical principles.

Assessment

Just as the same curriculum can be taught in a wide variety of ways, so it can also be assessed in lots of different ways. This includes **informally**, such as through in-lesson questioning and practice, and more **formally**, such as through end-of-topic tests and exams.[16]

Effectively, the term *assessment* is synonymous with 'checking'. We use informal and formal assessment approaches to check the extent to which something has been understood or learned.

---

11 Kirschner, P.A. and Hendrick, C. (2020) *How Learning Happens*
12 Kirschner, P.A., Sweller, J. and Clark, R.E. (2010) 'Why minimal guidance during instruction does not work'
13 Rosenshine, B. (2012) 'Principles of Instruction'
14 Robertson, B. (2020) *The Teaching Delusion*
15 Ibid
16 Robertson, B. (2021) *The Teaching Delusion 2*

It is important to draw a distinction between 'understanding' and 'learning' because they aren't necessarily the same thing. We can **understand** something as it is being taught but not **learn** it, because we no longer understand the same thing two days later (the result of diminishing memory strength).[17] Accepting this, **in-the-moment checks for understanding** *and* **longer-term checks for learning** should *both* be viewed as essential features of effective teaching. Hence, it can be helpful to think of assessment in short, medium and long-term cycles:[18]

Short cycle	After seconds, minutes or hours
Medium cycle	After days or weeks
Long cycle	After months or years

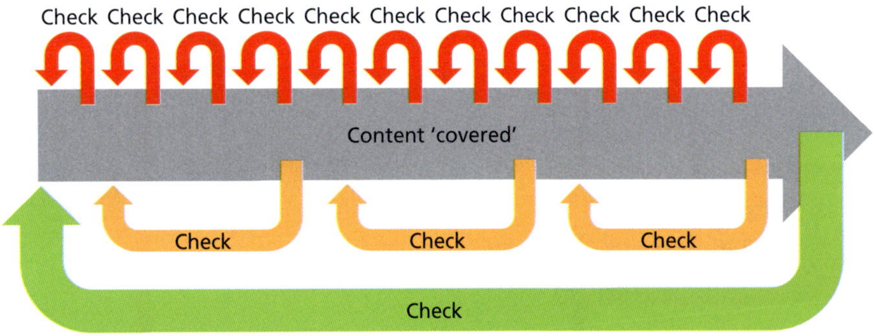

For a fuller exploration of this theme, see Appendix 2: An overview of assessment principles.

The overlap between curriculum, pedagogy and assessment

While drawing a distinction between *curriculum*, *pedagogy* and *assessment* can help to make it clear what we mean by these terms, in reality there is often overlap between them.

17 Brown, P.C., Roediger III, H.L. and McDaniel, M.A. (2014) *Make It Stick*
18 Wiliam, D. (2018) *Creating the Schools Our Children Need*

The overlap between curriculum and pedagogy

For example, if students are learning about Indian culture through reading, they should be developing **both** their knowledge of this topic and their reading skills.[19] If students are learning about the same topic via an interactive teacher presentation (no less valuable a teaching approach), they should be developing their knowledge of this topic but they won't be developing their reading skills. How content is taught can affect what is learned, hence the curriculum–pedagogy overlap:[20]

19 Of course, there are never any guarantees. Hence the importance of assessment (checking).

20 This is why some people talk about the 'intended curriculum' (that on paper) and the 'enacted curriculum' (that which is delivered to students). For example: https://my.chartered.college/impact_article/curriculum-reform-and-teacher-agency-how-national-policy-translates-to-the-classroom (Accessed: 12 March 2026)

The overlap between pedagogy and assessment

The overlap between pedagogy and assessment is generally more pronounced than that between curriculum and pedagogy. Indeed, because short, medium and long-term assessment should be viewed as integral features of effective teaching, there is a strong case to be made that assessment *is* pedagogy.[21]

As you would expect from the title of this book, while we will make occasional references to pedagogy and assessment, for the most part, we will be focusing on curriculum – the 'what' of teaching.

21 An exception might be final exams because teachers usually don't get sight of students' answers in these, meaning they can't be used to inform future teaching.

Focused reflection

- What are your key takeaways from this section?
- If you are a teacher or leader, are there any implications for your teaching or leadership?
- If you are a parent, what questions might you have for your child's school in relation to the points being made?

How good is your curriculum?

Having taken time to unpack what we mean by the *curriculum* (the 'what' of teaching) and differentiate this from *pedagogy* (the 'how') and *assessment* ('checking' understanding and learning), let's move on to consider another key question: **How good is the curriculum in your team or school?**

To get started, take a moment to consider the most relevant question:

Teacher	Middle leader	Senior leader
On a scale of 1–10, how good do you feel the curriculum is for the subject or year stage you teach, and why?	On a scale of 1–10, how good do you feel the curriculum is for the areas you are responsible for, and why?	On a scale of 1–10, how good do you feel the curriculum is across your school, and why?

How clear are you about the content?

To answer any of those questions with any confidence or certainty, you first need to have clarity about the detail of your curriculum. What knowledge and skills should students be learning, and what experiences should they be having? **How clear are you about this?**

Content clarity underpins purposeful pedagogy

One of the reasons these are all such important questions to consider is because everything stems from the curriculum. Before we can make decisions about teaching approaches (and assessment), we first need to be clear about what we want students to learn.[22] **Curriculum clarity underpins purposeful pedagogy.**

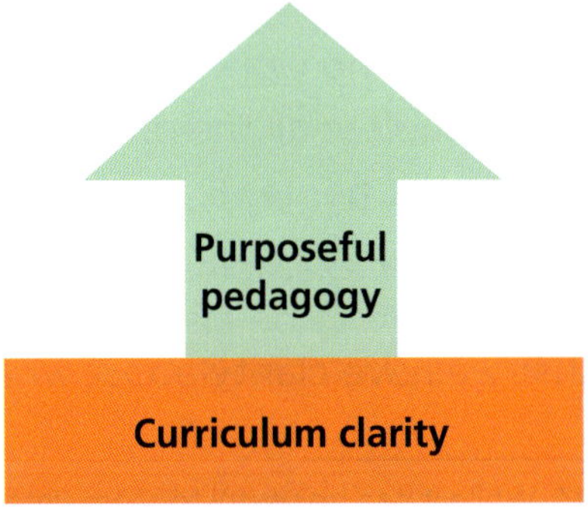

22 Sherrington, T. (2017) *The Learning Rainforest*

For example, teachers who are clear about what they want students to learn are far more likely to develop learning intentions and success criteria that look like these...

Learning intention (What we are aiming to learn)	Success criteria (The evidence to prove your learning)
We are learning about the **gunpower plot**; specifically, the reasons why it failed.	I can... describe *at least* two reasons why the gunpowder plot failed.
We are learning about the **digestive system**; specifically, to understand the structure of the digestive system.	I can... list the six most important parts. I can... label a diagram to name the six most important parts. I can... describe the order of the parts food moves through when in the digestive system.
We are learning to **swim front crawl**; specifically, to be able to perform an efficient leg kick.	When doing this, your: • legs will be straight and toes pointed • legs will reach a depth of approximately 18 inches and will create a bubble only at the surface • legs will pass close together • body position will be flat and will not rotate.

... than like these...

- Finish the worksheet you started in the last lesson.
- Complete all the problems on pages 55 to 56.
- Read Chapter 6 and discuss it with a partner.[23]

The former examples focus on *learning* and *evidence* of this, while the latter focus on *activities*. While we do need to be clear about the activities we want students to engage with, it is even more important that we have clarity about what we want students to learn as a result of engaging with them, and what

23 While it can be useful to share details of lesson activities with students, we need to be careful not to conflate **activities** with **learning**.

evidence we need to see or hear to get assurances learning is happening. Just because students are busy, doesn't mean they are learning. Hence, it can be useful to draw a distinction between **'being busy' activities** (that keep students occupied but do little to move learning forward) and **'learning' activities** (that develop new knowledge and skills).[24]

'Being busy' activities

To help illustrate this point, let's consider an example lesson.

The USA jigsaw:

In a geography lesson for 12-year-olds, students are put into groups of four. Each group is given a 'USA jigsaw' worksheet, showing the 50 states of America as jumbled jigsaw pieces.

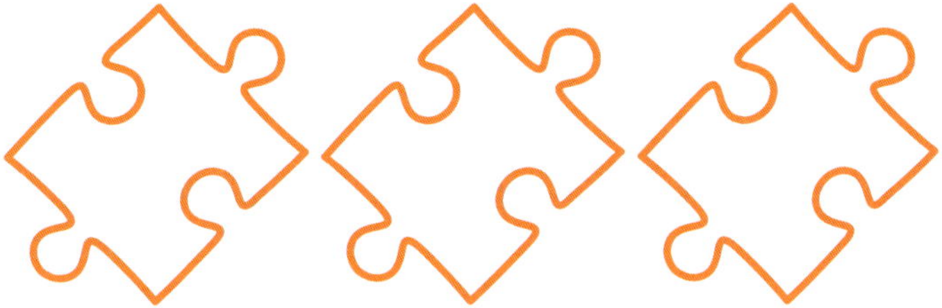

Groups are told they have 30 minutes to cut out the pieces and put the jigsaw together, which every group does successfully in the allotted time. Everyone is focused on the task at hand, behaving well, and most students appear to be enjoying what they are doing. All of which is good – **but what were they learning?**

24 Robertson, B. (2023) *Power Up Your Pedagogy*

To help find this out, the teacher uses an 'exit ticket' plenary.[25] Everyone is given a sheet of paper and asked to write a response to the question: What did you learn today? As students leave the room, the teacher collects the responses, reviewing them ahead of the next lesson.[26] Common responses include:

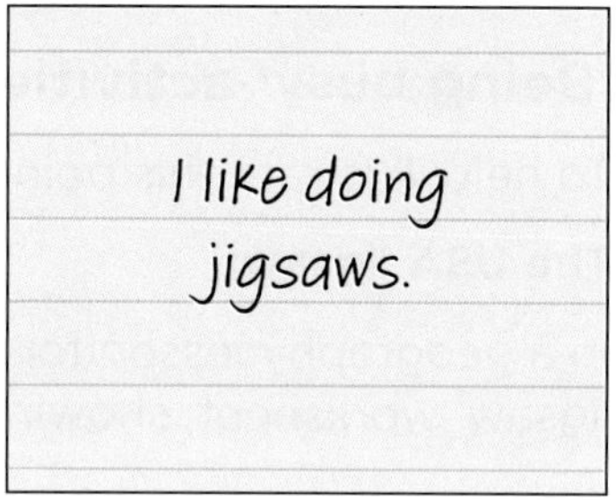

Was there learning? A little. Was this valuable? Arguably not. Was this the learning the teacher intended? Almost certainly not.

Discussing the lesson with a colleague over coffee, the teacher was very honest in their reflections. 'I know why I got so many exit tickets looking like that,' they said. 'I just wasn't clear in my own mind about what I wanted students to learn, so the task wasn't focused on clear learning goals. I had a loose idea that I wanted students to develop an awareness of where different states are in relation to one another, but I realise now that was just too vague. If I had been clearer in my own mind about the specific things I wanted students to learn, I would have planned an activity that was better for helping students to focus on and think about these things.'

25 Lemov, D. (2021) *Teach Like A Champion 3.0*

26 This can be a useful pedagogical technique, with evidence of understanding (or learning) from this lesson guiding the teacher's planning of the next lesson. The teacher could also have done this in other ways, for example using show-me boards.

Thinking is the key to learning

The latter part of the teacher's reflection is important, linking to a key message from cognitive science and educational research about how learning happens: **memory is the residue of thought**.[27] If we want students to learn particular things, we need to get them to **think** about these things. Thinking is the best bet we have when it comes to learning. **What is this activity most likely to get students to think about?** is therefore a key question for all teachers to keep at the forefront of their mind.

But of course, to help ensure students are thinking about the things we want them to learn, we first need to be clear about what these things are. Hence, the importance of a clear curriculum.

Focused reflection

- What are your key takeaways from this section?
- If you are a teacher or leader, are there any implications for your teaching or leadership?
- If you are a parent, what questions might you have for your child's school in relation to the points being made?

27 Willingham, D.T. (2010) *Why Don't Students Like School?*

Who should create the curriculum?

As we have explored the themes to this point, if you are a teacher, you might reasonably have been thinking: 'I'm not really sure why we are spending time on this. It's my job to **teach** the curriculum in the best way possible – I shouldn't have to be planning it as well.' If that's the case, I'm with you. There are at least three reasons why.

The barrier of time

The first reason relates to the reality of school life. Many teachers in many schools simply don't have the time to focus on curriculum creation **and** everything else they are expected to do (such as plan and deliver lessons, plan and mark assessments, maintain tracking records, report to parents, lead clubs, respond to emails, attend meetings, engage with professional development... and a lot more besides). If we are going to ask teachers to create the curriculum, **blocks of time need to be ring-fenced** for them to do this, and some other things will almost certainly need to go.

The barrier of subject knowledge

The second reason relates to teachers' subject knowledge. If we are being honest, many teachers simply don't have sufficient subject knowledge to be able to create a great curriculum (that's not intended to be a criticism; it's just a fact). I can relate to this fully. While I know I could plan a curriculum of sorts for the subjects I am qualified to teach, I also know there are a lot of other people who could create a curriculum that is a lot better than the one that I could create. One of the reasons is that they have better subject knowledge then me, which I'm perfectly happy to acknowledge. Give me details of the curriculum I am to teach and I will get my subject knowledge up to speed in any areas required, but I need to be given a clear curriculum first.

The risk of inequity between schools

The third reason is that the more we devolve curriculum creation to schools, the more likely the quality of curriculum will vary widely from school to school. Some schools will likely develop excellent curricula; some will develop curricula that are good; some will develop curricula that aren't very good at all. This results in **inequity in students' learning** from the moment they set foot through the school door. Regardless of how well teachers are teaching, some students are going to get a curriculum that is better than others. Had students who are being taught a poor (or average) curriculum gone to a school teaching a great curriculum, they would almost certainly have learned and achieved more. Probably, a *lot* more. To me, that isn't okay. **All students** should have access to a high-quality curriculum, regardless of the school they attend.

National vs local curriculum decisions

Of all the points above, it is likely to be the last that stokes the most discussion and debate. Schools that have taken time to create their own excellent curriculum are unlikely to be happy if they are told to abandon this and conform with a standardised national curriculum, particularly if they view this as sub-standard to what they have created themselves. I have some sympathy with this position.

The sweet spot

While one of the surest ways to ensure equity of education for all **is** to have a common, detailed national curriculum for everyone, the reality is there are limits to the degree of specification many teachers and schools are willing to accept.[28] With that in mind, the most sensible approach to curriculum creation can probably be found in the sweet spot of a **curriculum creation spectrum**:

---

28 Paterson, L. (2026) *Lessons from Scottish Schools*

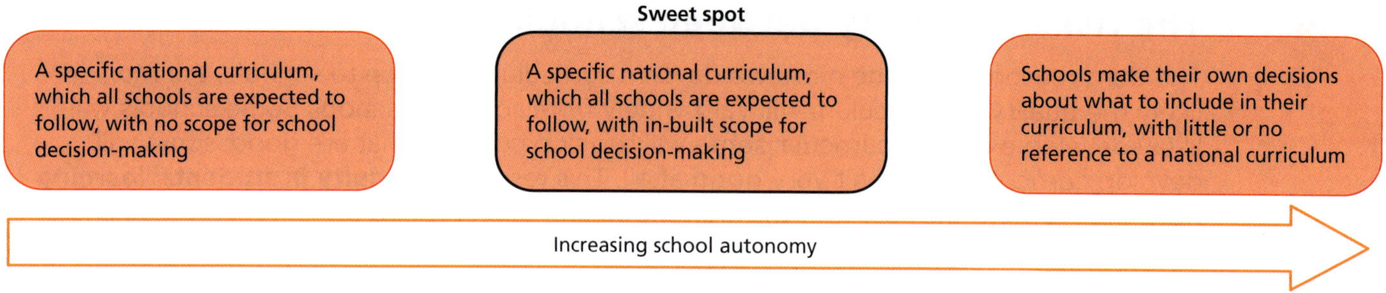

This sweet spot aims to strike **a balance between national consistency and local autonomy**, with both professional acceptability and student equity in mind. For example, a national curriculum might specify a suite of books, from which schools can make their own choices. Importantly, schools should be able to go beyond this suite. This principle should apply to knowledge, skills and experiences across all subject areas. However, the important point to restress is that the more autonomy schools have, the more we risk inequity as a result of variations in quality.[29]

Focused reflection

- What are your key takeaways from this section?
- If you are a teacher or leader, are there any implications for your teaching or leadership?
- If you are a parent, what questions might you have for your child's school in relation to the points being made?

29 Hence, the increasing weight to the argument that the quality of a school's curriculum should be evaluated by external bodies, such as national inspectors.

Part 2: Curriculum Concepts

Curriculum Concept 1: Skills are knowledge in action

Curriculum Concept 2: Knowledge is the catalyst to understanding and future learning

Curriculum Concept 3: The more specific a skill, the more likely it can be taught directly, and the more likely it can be transferred

Curriculum Concept 4: The best way to teach meta-skills is to focus on knowledge

Curriculum Concept 5: When developing your curriculum, start with the big picture and work your way in

Curriculum Concept 6: Power up your curriculum using 5Cs

Curriculum Concept 1: Skills are knowledge in action

Common pitfall: We think of knowledge and skills as being in competition with each other.

The knowledge vs skills battle

Often in education, the very mention of 'knowledge' gets some people hot under the collar. These are usually people who think of knowledge as being old-fashioned and out-dated, and who say things such as:

- 'Students don't need knowledge any more – they can just look everything up online or use AI.'
- 'Schools should be focusing on teaching skills.'
- 'Transferable skills should be the focus of a 21st century education.'[30]

People who think like this seem to be imagining knowledge and skills on opposing sides of a curriculum battle, with skills the goodie and knowledge the baddie.

30 Sometimes, 'transferable skills' is replaced with '21st-century skills' or 'meta-skills'.

However, this battle is an unnecessary one. Knowledge and skills aren't enemies – they're actually very good friends. **Skills are knowledge in action.**[31]

Let's explore this further, starting with an overview of how learning happens.

How learning happens

The following diagram summarises the way everyone learns:

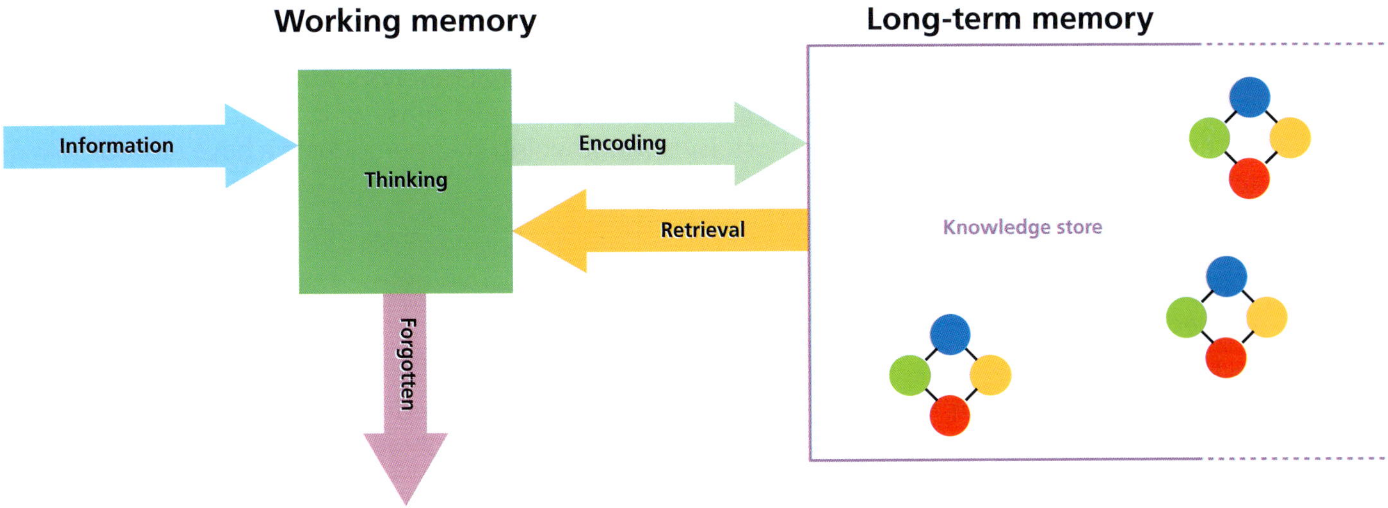

31 Robertson, B. (2021) *The Teaching Delusion 2*

Working memory and long-term memory

When information comes to our attention – things that we see or hear – it enters **working memory** first. Working memory is where **thinking** can happen. However, we tend not to think about most of what we see or hear for particularly long or hard. For that reason, most of the information that enters working memory falls out relatively quickly. In other words, it is **forgotten**.

However, not everything falls out of working memory in this way. Sometimes, there is transfer from working memory to long-term memory – **encoding** – and this initiates the learning process.[32] **Learning is the development of long-term memory.**

The reason we develop long-term memory is that it serves an essential function. When we see or hear new information, we **retrieve** the content of long-term memory to make sense of it. Sometimes, this is automatic; other times, it requires deliberate effort. By strengthening the memories we have stored, retrieval plays an important role in the learning process too.[33]

Knowledge

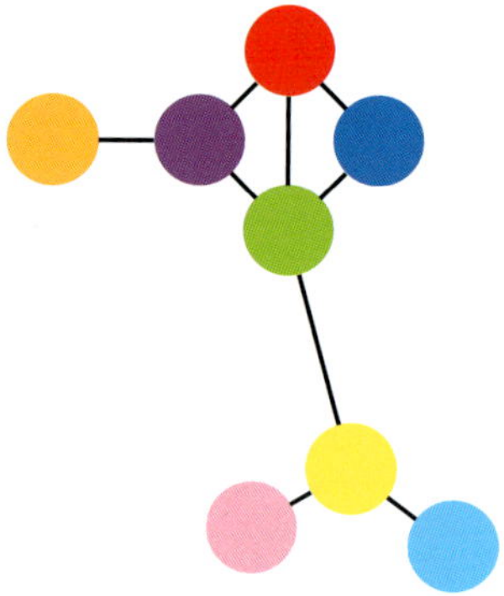

We store information in long-term memory as **knowledge** in connected constructs called schema.

Some of the knowledge we store in schema is **declarative** – of facts and concepts, which we can articulate, verbally or in writing; some of it is **procedural** – knowledge of how to do things, which we can't necessarily articulate, but we can demonstrate. Here are some examples:

32 Heal, J. and Berlin, R. (2025) *Mental Models*

33 The principle that retrieval strengthens memory is often referred to as the 'Testing Effect', for example see Brown, P.C., Roediger III, H.L. and McDaniel, M.A. (2014) *Make It Stick*

Subject	Declarative knowledge	Procedural knowledge
English	What we mean by 'verbs'	Identifying verbs in sentences
Science	Why it is important to balance chemical equations	How to balance chemical equations
PE	The rules of basketball	How to perform an effective layup in basketball

Depending on the nature of the subject we are teaching or the particular lesson at hand, the focus might be more on one type of knowledge or the other. Regardless, everything we store in long-term memory is knowledge. Skills are the application of this knowledge. Hence, the 'cognitive architecture' model applies to all subjects.

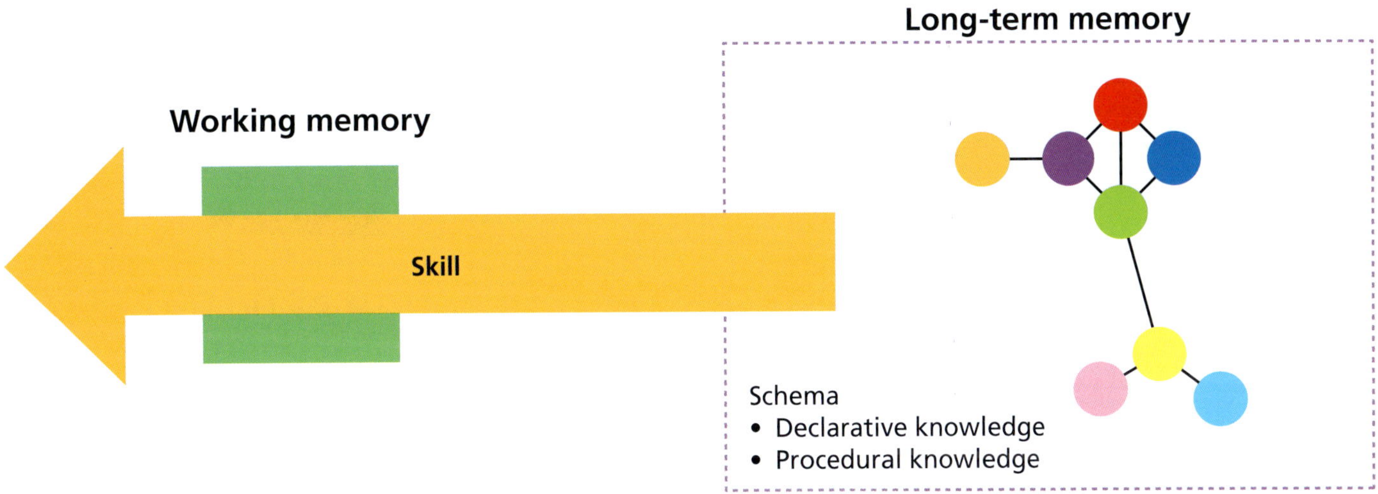

Knowledge-based and skills-orientated

Accepting this, it doesn't really make sense to think of some subjects as being 'knowledge-based' and others 'skills-based'. **All subjects are knowledge-based and skills-orientated.**

In some subjects (or lessons), the focus might be more on teaching declarative knowledge than procedural knowledge. In others, the opposite might be true. Regardless: knowledge is the bedrock of all learning. Students apply this knowledge as skill.

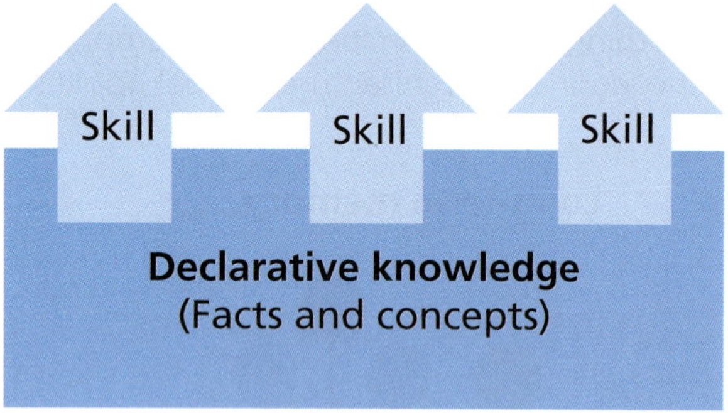

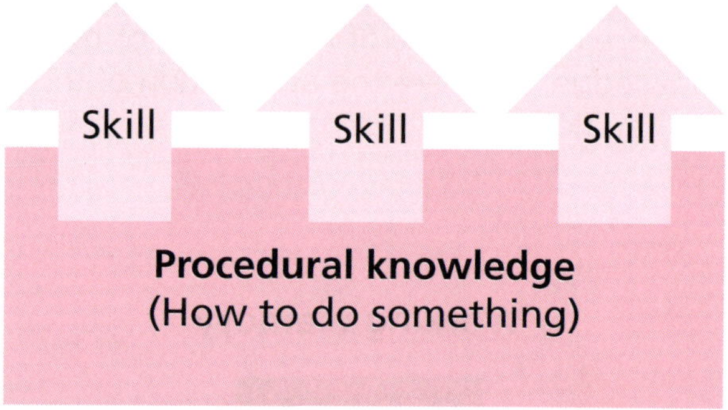

For example:

- In a literacy lesson, students might be taught **declarative knowledge** about what adjectives are and why they are important. They might then be given the opportunity to identify adjectives in sentences – a **skill** – and to write sentences that include adjectives – a different **skill**.
- In a maths lesson, students might be taught **declarative and procedural knowledge** about what quadrilaterals are and how to identify them, including via a definition and examples. They might then be asked to identify shapes that could be classified as quadrilaterals – a **skill** – and draw a range of examples themselves – a different **skill**.
- In a PE lesson, students might be taught **procedural knowledge** about effective layups in basketball via a teacher demonstration. They might then be asked to put this knowledge into action via deliberate practice – a **skill** – and to critique the quality of layups being practised by their peers – a different **skill**.

What a knowledge-based curriculum is and isn't

A 'facts-only curriculum'

Sometimes, when people hear the phrase 'knowledge-based', they think of a curriculum that focuses on facts, better suited to helping students win quizzes than equipping them to flourish in the wider world. However, this **isn't** what we mean by a knowledge-based curriculum. There is a huge difference between students memorising random, unconnected facts and them **building large, interconnected webs of knowledge** that help them to make sense of the world and think for themselves. A knowledge-based curriculum isn't a 'facts-only curriculum'.[34]

---

34 Which isn't to say students shouldn't be taught facts – of course they should. We're simply saying a knowledge-based curriculum should go far beyond this, developing students' understanding of principles, concepts and a lot more besides.

An 'exams-focused curriculum'

Nor is a knowledge-based curriculum an 'exams-focused curriculum'. True, in the latter years of school, many students will sit exams. However, the curriculum they are taught in both the proceeding and examination years should focus on much more than the knowledge needed to pass exams. This knowledge is obviously important, but it shouldn't be thought of as exclusive.

At the extreme, an overemphasis on knowledge needed to pass exams leads to students saying such things as, 'Why are we spending time on this if it's not in the exam?' and teachers justifying what they are teaching because of exams. This includes with year groups who aren't even in an examination year. 'You need to learn this because in three years' time you might be examined on it' is a very sad phrase to hear any teacher using. Most of the things we teach students at school should be seen to have value in themselves, by teachers and students, because they might be useful or interesting – not just necessary to get a good grade.

A 'thinking curriculum'

A knowledge-based curriculum **is** a 'thinking curriculum'. **Knowledge is thinking fuel** – without it, we can't think.

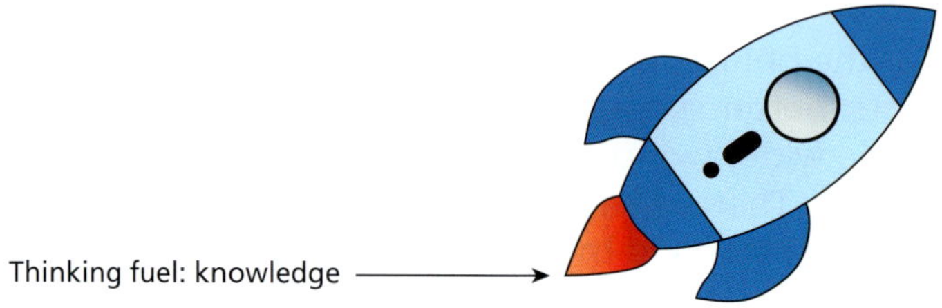

In *Creating The Schools Our Children Need*, Dylan Wiliam captures this neatly:

> The main purpose of the curriculum is to build up the content of long-term memory so that when students are asked to think, they are able to think in more powerful ways because what is in their long-term memories makes their [working memories] more powerful.[35]

At its core, teaching in schools should focus on helping students to develop declarative and procedural knowledge in long-term memory, complemented with opportunities for this to be applied in structured and unstructured ways as skills.

Does this apply to all year groups, including Early Years?

The cognitive architecture model we have discussed applies to all subjects, but does it apply to all year groups, including Early Years?

To answer this, we should turn our attention to a conversation between Tom Sherrington, Emma Turner and Dylan Wiliam in the excellent *Mind The Gap* podcast. As part of a discussion, Dylan Wiliam is asked whether the cognitive architecture model applies to the youngest students we are teaching.[36] His answer is yes. Fundamentally, the way a four-year-old thinks and learns isn't that different from how a ten-year-old or sixteen-year-old thinks and learns. The relationship between working memory and long-term memory is the same and is key.

---

35 Wiliam, D. (2018) *Creating the Schools Our Children Need*

36 www.youtube.com/watch?v=7ynsMwzsCsg (Accessed: 26 March 2026)

That said, there are three caveats to keep in mind.

Caveat 1

The first is that it can be more challenging to get younger children to pay attention to the things we need them to – that is, **to get information into working memory** in the first place. Our teaching needs to take account of this.[37]

Caveat 2

The second is that the **working-memory capacity** of younger children is smaller than those who are older, meaning they can't hold and think about as much at one time.[38] Our teaching needs to take account of this, too.

Caveat 3

The third relates to the difference between **biologically primary knowledge** and **biologically secondary knowledge**,[39] which can be summarised as follows:

	Biologically primary knowledge	Biologically secondary knowledge
Meaning	Knowledge that humans are programmed to acquire automatically	Knowledge that humans aren't programmed to acquire automatically
Examples	Talking, listening, socialising and generalising	Reading, writing, maths and most of what we want students to learn in all subjects
Teaching	Can't be taught directly and should be developed through experiences	Can and should be taught directly

37 Willingham, D.T. (2010) *Why Don't Students Like School?*
38 https://evidencebased.education/resource/how-limited-is-working-memory-capacity (Accessed: 26 March 2026)
39 Geary, D.C. (1995) 'Reflections of Evolution and Culture in Children's Cognition' (see Ashman, G. [2023] *Cognitive Load Theory*)

The relationship between working memory (thinking) and long-term memory (storing) needn't be as important a consideration when it comes to the development of biologically primary knowledge, but it should be one of the most important considerations for all the biologically secondary knowledge we are teaching students, including those who are the youngest.[40]

Focused reflection

- What are your key takeaways from this section?
- If you are a teacher or leader, are there any implications for your teaching or leadership?
- If you are a parent, what questions might you have for your child's school in relation to the points being made?

40 Ashman, G. (2023) *Cognitive Load Theory*

Curriculum Concept 2: Knowledge is the catalyst to understanding and future learning

Common pitfall: We don't believe students need knowledge anymore, because they can just look everything up online or use AI.

Knowledge in the 21st century

As tempting as it might be to believe we can outsource knowledge to online platforms and technology – meaning students don't need to learn things anymore because they can just look them up – this sort of thinking is a big mistake.[41] There are at least three reasons why:

1. Looking things up slows everything down.
2. We can't understand specific things unless we know specific things.
3. The more we know, the more we are likely to know in future.

We shall take time to explore each of these reasons.

41 Christodoulou, D. (2013) *Seven Myths About Education*

1. Looking things up slows everything down

The first reason is that every time we have to look something up (for example, by using a search engine), we slow everything else down. This is true even if we find the thing we are looking for relatively quickly, but worse if we can't find the thing we are looking for at all.

For example, imagine a student is reading the following news article:

> Water companies have been ordered to tackle potentially harmful levels of so-called forever chemicals in drinking-water sources for more than six million people. Forever chemicals, or PFAS, are a group of thousands of substances used in everyday products. They are persistent pollutants that build up in the environment, and a small number have been linked to increased risk of some serious illnesses.[42]

In the first sentence, they get stuck on the meanings of *tackle* and *potentially*. This puts immediate brakes on their progress. To try to find out what these words mean, they use an online search engine. This brings us to the second reason why it is a mistake to outsource knowledge...

2. We can't understand specific things unless we know specific things

Although the student has been able to use the search engine to find definitions of the words they are stuck on, the extent to which they can understand these will depend on what they already know (in other words, what they have stored in their long-term memory).

42 www.bbc.co.uk/news/articles/c9q1nzyzyjeo (Accessed: 26 March 2026)

For *tackle*, the search engine gives them the following information:

Noun

1. the equipment required for a task or sport
2. a mechanism consisting of ropes, pulley blocks, hooks or other things for lifting heavy objects

Verb

1. make determined efforts to deal with (a problem or difficult task)
2. try to take the ball from (an opponent) by intercepting them[43]

With four options to choose from and a lack of knowledge about whether they are dealing with a noun or a verb, the student is none the wiser about the meaning of *tackle* in this article.

Giving up on this, they look up the word *potentially*. This time, they get the following information:

Adverb

with the capacity to develop or happen in the future[44]

They ignore *adverb*, because they're not sure what that means, but then immediately get stuck again because they're not sure what *capacity* means either. Persevering, they decide to look this up as well and get the following:

Noun

1. the maximum amount that something can contain
2. the amount that something can produce
3. a specified role or position[45]

---

43 Oxford dictionary online
44 Ibid
45 Ibid

Stumped by which of these three is the correct meaning in this context, they give up altogether and decide to spend time on Instagram instead.

Understanding is remembering in disguise

While it is true that search engines and AI can be useful in helping to **find information**, the extent to which anything found will be **understood** depends on the content of our long-term memory. When we see or hear things, we retrieve knowledge from long-term memory to make sense of this.[46] The extent to which we can make sense of and think about anything depends on what we have stored in long-term memory. This is the reason Daniel Willingham has suggested that **understanding is remembering in disguise**.[47]

If students are to be able to think critically about the information they find using the internet and AI, including to evaluate the extent to which this is accurate and to form opinions, they need **knowledge stored in long-term memory to think with**.[48] The more knowledge students have, the more likely they are to pause and think, 'Hang on a minute, that doesn't seem right' or 'I'm not sure I agree with that because…'. Students with less knowledge to think with are more likely to accept everything they read as facts, even when these might be wrong. Because people are getting their information from the internet and AI more and more, and because not everything they read will be true, now – more than ever – schools need to empower students by developing rich pools of knowledge they can draw upon from long-term memory.

---

46 Willingham, D.T. (2006) 'How Knowledge Helps'
47 Willingham, D.T. (2010) *Why Don't Students Like School?*
48 Lennard, E. (2025) 'Building A Strong Knowledge-Rich Curriculum'

Higher-order thinking

That is the reason Dylan Wiliam has suggested that 'Bloom's Taxonomy', so often referred to in education and represented as a pyramid...[49]

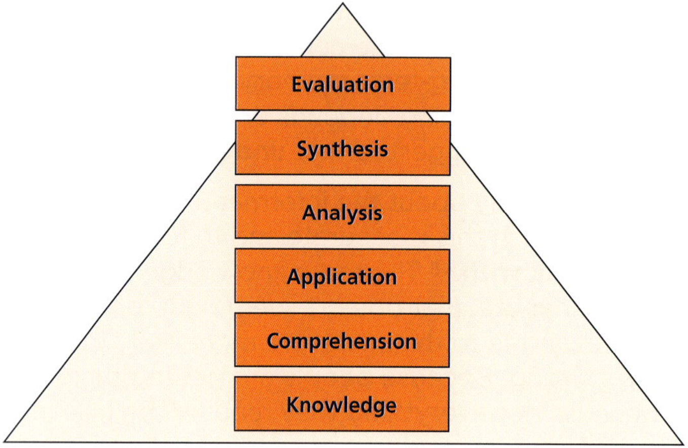

... would be better thought of and represented like this...

49 Note: Benjamin Bloom didn't present learning as pyramid – the pyramid has been created subsequently by others, as discussed in Hendrick C. and Macpherson, R. (2017) *What Does This Look Like In The Classroom?*

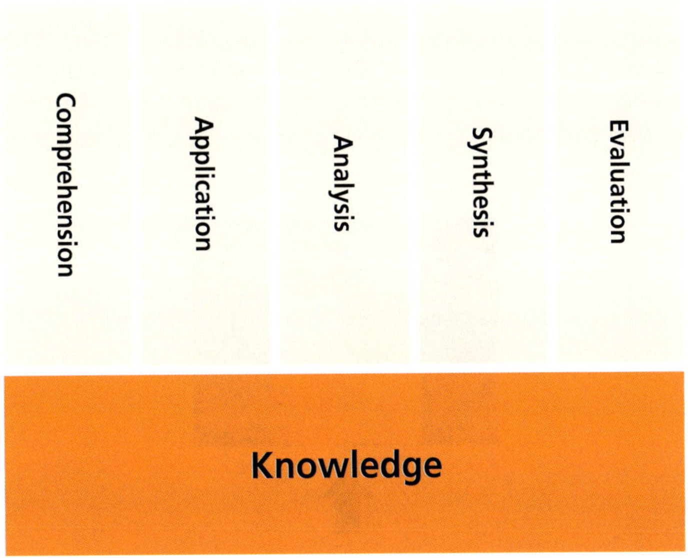

Students can't engage in 'higher-order' thinking unless they have 'lower-order' knowledge to think with. Knowledge is the bedrock of all thinking and is the pre-condition for every higher-order skill society values.[50]

50 Wiliam, D. (2025) 'Knowledge-Rich Curricula'

Building blocks

Every piece of knowledge we teach students at school functions as a building block to something bigger.[51] The 'something bigger' is usually more valuable than each smaller block, but the blocks are nonetheless essential to get there. This is why memorisation is a necessary step to the development of more powerful knowledge.[52]

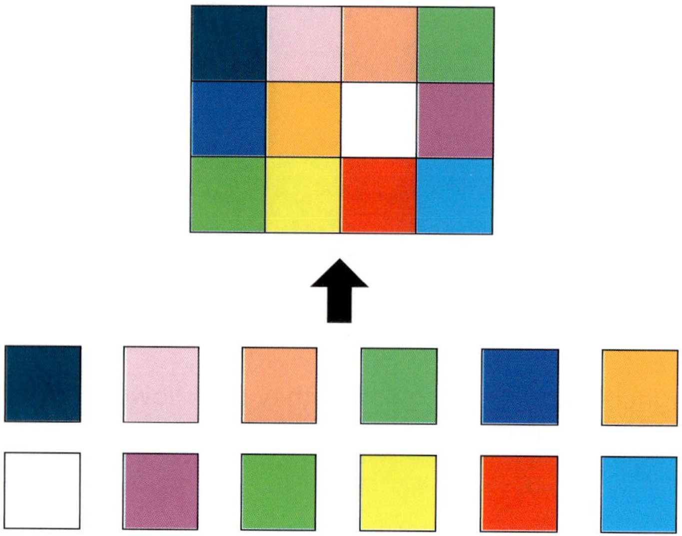

51 Robertson, B. (2021) *The Teaching Delusion 2*
52 Young, M. (2020) 'From Powerful Knowledge To The Powers Of Knowledge'

For example, knowledge of the meaning of *evaporation* is a building block to understanding the bigger concept of why puddles 'disappear'. The meaning of *evaporation* (and many other facts) needs to be learned before deeper understanding can develop.

Mental mosaics

A good analogy is mosaics, which are pieces of art created from smaller coloured stones. The stones have some value in themselves, but it is the art they come together to create that has the most value. A core purpose of school is to help students develop their own 'metal mosaics' from building blocks of core knowledge. At times, the blocks being learned might seem pointless. However, in the longer term, the more blocks students have, the more impressive the mosaic they will be able to create. As we shall go on to discuss later in this book, critical-thinking, problem-solving and creativity - all forms of mental mosaics - all require knowledge blocks.

Rote knowledge, shallow knowledge and deep knowledge

Before we move on, we should take a moment to add one important cautionary note. While memorisation is important, this should always be accompanied with **at least some degree of understanding** of what is being memorised. Students being able to recall something doesn't mean they understand it.[53] The best way to check the extent to which something has been understood is to check the extent it can be **transferred to unfamiliar situations** or **applied in new ways**.

In *Why Don't Students Like School?*, Daniel Willingham discusses this principle by drawing attention to three hierarchical levels of knowledge:[54]

---

53 Kirschner, P.A., Hendrick, C. and Heal, J. (2022) *How Teaching Happens*
54 Willingham, D.T. (2010) *Why Don't Students Like School?*

	Meaning	Example
Rote knowledge	Students know something but lack accompanying understanding, meaning they can't apply this knowledge.	They have learned the definition of a molecule and can repeat this back, word-for-word. However, they can't identify molecules from formulae or diagrams.
Shallow knowledge	Students know something and have some accompanying understanding, meaning they can apply this knowledge, but in a limited way.	They have learned the definition of a molecule and can identify *some* molecules from formulae and diagrams, but not with consistent accuracy.
Deep knowledge	Students know something and have a lot of accompanying understanding, meaning they can apply this knowledge widely.	They have learned the definition of a molecule and can identify molecules from formulae and diagrams consistently accurately. More than this, they can provide their own examples of formulae and diagrams of molecules, and explain what a molecule is in their own words.

Ultimately, schools should be aiming to develop **deep knowledge**. However, to get there, we often need to work through the rote and shallow levels first.

Pointless rote knowledge

The word *often* is important in the previous sentence. Forcing students to learn by rote when they don't need to do this is not good teaching. To help illustrate this point, consider the following anecdote that I shared in *The Teaching Delusion 2*:

> I once observed a lesson that began with an activity in which students were asked to look up the dictionary definition of four words and copy these out. The idea was that, by doing so, they would learn their meaning. One student put up their hand and said, 'I already know what these words mean.' The teacher quizzed him: 'Okay, so what does *disingenuous* mean?' The student gave what to me was a good explanation of this word. 'That's good,' said the teacher, 'but I want you to learn the dictionary definition.' My look of bemusement was bettered only by that of the student.[55]

55 Robertson, B. (2021) *The Teaching Delusion 2*

The student didn't need to learn the dictionary definition – he already had a good understanding of what *disingenuous* means. A far better use of his time would have been to engage in activities that helped consolidate and extend his understanding, for example, by trying to use the word in three different sentences, or to list as many synonyms of the word as he could.

3. The more we know, the more we are likely to know in future

A third reason that outsourcing knowledge to online platforms and technology is a mistake is because of a principle often referred to as the 'Matthew Effect': people who know more are in a better position to learn more in future.[56]

The importance of connection

The 'Matthew Effect' principle is rooted in the way leaning happens: new knowledge is acquired by making connections to the existing knowledge we have stored in schema in long-term memory:

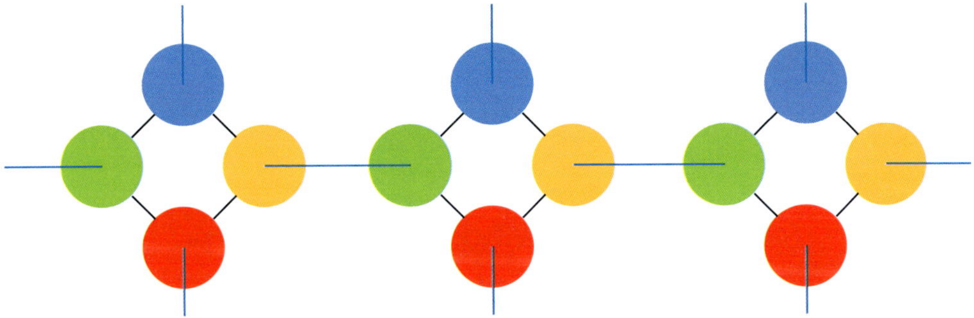

56 Willingham, D.T. (2006) 'How Knowledge Helps'

The more knowledge we have in a schema, the more opportunities there are for new connections, and the more likely new learning will happen.[57]

Snowballs

A useful analogy is a snowball rolling down a hill. Just as bigger snowballs will get bigger more quickly as they roll, so it is with learning. People who have more knowledge (declarative or procedural) are more likely to learn **even more**. The opposite is true for anyone with less knowledge.

This is why E.D. Hirsch has suggested the internet mainly rewards people who have a lot of knowledge stored in long-term memory:

> Google is not an equal-opportunity fact finder; it rewards those already in the know.[58]

57 https://link.springer.com/book/10.1007/978-3-031-74661-1 (Accessed: 26 March 2026)
58 Hirsch, E.D. (2016) *Why Knowledge Matters*

A link to pedagogy and gaps

The attainment gap

The 'Matthew Effect' principle also has important implications for pedagogy and our drive to close attainment gaps, as Paul Kirscher, Carl Hendrick and Jim Heal make clear:

> Discovery approaches (such as trying to learn something new by searching online), if and when they occasionally work, often advantage students who **already possess substantial background knowledge** and metacognitive skills, typically those from more privileged backgrounds, while disadvantaging precisely those students most in need of explicit instruction.[59]

This is the reason so much educational literature suggests a **knowledge-based curriculum is the best shot we have of overcoming educational inequalities linked to background circumstances**.[60] If some students have access to rich pools of knowledge at home and others don't, the students with this access have a learning advantage from the get-go. The achievement gap is really a knowledge gap.[61]

The experience gap

Building on this, I would suggest that the **experience gap** (which doesn't get discussed nearly as often) is as important a consideration. It isn't right that some students get access to great literature and cultural experiences at home while others don't. Nor is it right that some students get the opportunity to learn to play the drums or tennis while others don't. In an equitable education, experience gaps matter as much as achievement gaps.

---

59 Kirschner, P.A., Hendrick, C. and Heal, J. (2025) *Instructional Illusions* (the emphasis is my own)

60 For example: Young, M. and Lambert, D. (2014) *Knowledge and the Future School*, Hirsch, E.D. (2016) *Why Knowledge Matters* and Wiliam, D. (2018) *Creating the Schools Our Children Need*

61 Hirsch, E.D. (2016) *Why Knowledge Matters*

The role schools can play

Schools can help address achievement and experience gaps between students from the most and least advantaged homes by making sure **all students** get access to the same **core content** through school.[62] By doing so, they can help level the playing field.

While it is unlikely schools will ever be able to make up for background inequalities completely, with social justice in mind there is a strong argument that 'access to knowledge, skills and experiences for all' should be thought of as the primary purpose of schooling.[63]

62 Hirsch, E.D. (2016) *Why Knowledge Matters*
63 Young, M. (2020) 'From Powerful Knowledge to the Powers of Knowledge'

The wrong direction

In educational systems where the focus has shifted from the systematic development of knowledge, achievement gaps between students from the most and least affluent homes have tended to increase.[64] The reason is that those from more affluent homes acquire much more knowledge at home than those from less affluent homes.[65] As Clare Sealy stresses:

> Where a curriculum removes content in the mistaken belief that this is a sure route to skills, it is the children with the lowest starting points who suffer the most. Conversely, a [knowledge-based] curriculum, taught well, provides the most inclusive kind of curriculum.[66]

The example of Scotland

This is precisely what has happened in Scotland in recent years as a result of the implementation of 'Curriculum for Excellence'.[67] At its core, this curriculum comprises several hundred 'Experiences and Outcomes' statements, such as the following examples:[68]

---

64 Robertson, B. (2021) *The Teaching Delusion 2*

65 Wiliam, D. (2025) 'Knowledge-rich curricula: A key driver of equity in education' in *The value of a knowledge-rich curriculum: An essay collection* [online] Available at: www.civitas.org.uk/publications/knowledge-rich-curriculum (Accessed: 26 March 2026)

66 Sealy, C. (2025) 'Knowledge And Skills: A Journey Not A Dichotomy' in *The value of a knowledge-rich curriculum: An essay collection* [online] Available at: www.civitas.org.uk/publications/knowledge-rich-curriculum (Accessed: 26 March 2026)

67 www.enlighten.scot/misleading-educational-statistics (Accessed: 26 March 2026)

68 https://auth.education.gov.scot/media/wpsnskgv/all-experiencesoutcomes18.pdf (Accessed: 26 March 2026)

English	Using what I know about the features of different types of texts, I can find, select and sort information from a variety of sources and use this for different purposes.
Maths	Having determined which calculations are needed, I can solve problems involving whole numbers using a range of methods, sharing my approaches and solutions with others.
Science	Through investigation, I can explain how changes in learned behaviour due to internal and external stimuli are of benefit to the survival of species.
History	I can describe the main features of conflicting world belief systems in the past and can present informed views on the consequences of such conflict for societies then and since.
Art	Through observing and recording from my experiences across the curriculum, I can create images and objects which show my awareness and recognition of detail.
Technologies	I can explore and comment on processes in the world around me making use of core computational thinking concepts and can organise information in a logical way.

Being honest, I find it hard to accept that this is a curriculum. The main reason is that it is incredibly difficult for anyone – teachers, leaders or parents – to understand **what students should be learning**, which is the very thing a curriculum should be making clear.[69] The curriculum has been reduced to end goals (outcomes) and pedagogies masquerading as experiences (such as 'research' and 'investigation') with little or no detail about what students should actually be learning.[70]

69 The thing a national curriculum doesn't need to be specifying – pedagogy – is the very thing often being specified in competency-based curricula. We shouldn't be seeing statements such as 'Through investigation' or 'By researching' – this is the 'how', not the 'what'.

70 Hence, these statements are referred to in national documentation as 'Experiences and Outcomes'.

As a result, different teachers in different schools looking at the same curriculum statements are very likely to make different interpretations as to what these mean in practice. This leads to the content of the curriculum varying wildly from school to school. To quote *The Teaching Delusion 2*:

> As written, this 'curriculum' is the equivalent of saying to a group of people, 'I want you to go to a city in Europe' and then expecting everyone to arrive at the same city. Actually, it's worse than that. It's more like: 'I want you to go to a section of land in the continent that lies somewhere between Asia and North America, which has lots of people in it, a significant number of buildings, and a wide variety of trees.' Let's not be too shocked when everyone ends up in a different place.[71]

A national-curriculum lottery

The impact of this on a national scale is that we create a **curriculum lottery**,[72] with some students in some schools experiencing a curriculum that is coherent and challenging, pushing them to learn and achieve the very best they can, and other students in other schools experiencing a curriculum that is fragmented and limiting, holding their learning back. Some students are taught extensive bodies of knowledge that develop cultural literacy and a deep understanding of the world beyond their local context – others don't get this chance. Some students become inspired to continue to learn about subjects and topics they never imagined they would be interested in had they not been introduced at school, while others won't. Differentiated curricula harm both achievement and equity.[73]

71 Robertson, B. (2021) *The Teaching Delusion 2*
72 https://link.springer.com/book/10.1007/978-3-031-74661-1 (Accessed: 26 March 2026)
73 Hirsch, E.D. (2016) *Why Knowledge Matters*

The importance of clear specification at a national level

As was argued in Part 1 of this book, with equity of achievement (and experience) in mind, there should be clear specification about **what *all students* should be taught in *all schools***, at least as a minimum, at a national level. The steer should be: '**Every student** going to **any school** will be taught about *this* and how to do *this*. **Everyone** will get the experience of *this*.'

For example, if nationally it is decided all students should learn about climate change or the causes of World War II, a national curriculum should make this clear. If it doesn't, we leave whether or not students learn anything about these things at school to chance. We then get scenarios such as those following playing out:

Students from Redhouse and Greenfield primary schools all go to Bluesky secondary school. The Redhouse primary-school curriculum includes **how the human heart works** and the **Scottish witch trials**. The Greenfield primary-school curriculum doesn't include either of these things. Neither primary school shares their curriculum with Bluesky secondary school, which doesn't share its curriculum with the primary schools either.

The Bluesky secondary-school curriculum doesn't include anything about the human heart, so most students who went to Greenfield primary school never learn anything about this at any stage, leaving secondary school without any knowledge of this topic. *Most* is important to highlight, because there are *some* students from Greenfield primary school who get to learn about how the human heart works, but this learning comes from resources and teaching at home, not from school.

The Bluesky secondary-school curriculum *does* include the Scottish witch trials. For students from Greenfield primary school who have never been taught anything about this previously, this is good.

> However, for students from Redhouse primary school, this doesn't prove nearly so valuable, because most students already knew everything that is being taught. While repetition is generally good for learning, this should be planned and deliberate. For students from Redhouse primary school, precious time that could have been used to learn new topics is squandered.

In my experience, the scenario outlined here is very common in Scottish education and is intrinsically linked to a lack of content clarity. Students have gaps in their learning because we don't know what they are being taught and they aren't being challenged in their learning for the same reason. Therefore, it should be little wonder that after a decade or more of trying, there has been minimal progress towards closing background-related achievement gaps.[74] A key reason is that no one has stepped up to lead the development of a clear knowledge-based, skills-orientated national curriculum.

Perfection can't be the enemy of good

While such a national curriculum is unlikely to be perfect, we can't let perfection be the enemy of good. Over time, the content of the curriculum can evolve and improve. But for that to happen, we need to start with **something**.

Focused reflection

- What are your key takeaways from this section?
- If you are a teacher or leader, are there any implications for your teaching or leadership?
- If you are a parent, what questions might you have for your child's school in relation to the points being made?

74 www.enlighten.scot/misleading-educational-statistics (Accessed: 26 March 2026)

Curriculum Concept 3: The more specific a skill, the more likely it can be taught directly, and the more likely it can be transferred

Common pitfall: We overgeneralise what we mean by 'skills', meaning we try to teach things that can't be taught directly.

How do we teach students skills?

Having explored what we mean by 'curriculum' (content) and the relationship between knowledge and skills, let's move on to consider a different question: **What is the best way to teach students skills?**

We will unpack this question over the course of Curriculum Concepts 3 and 4.

Classifying skills

Let's start with a thinking task.

From the following options, which would you classify as 'skills'?

- Critical-thinking
- Motivation
- Summarising the main idea of a message
- Resilience
- Using full stops in a sentence
- Problem-solving
- Creativity
- Communication
- Collaboration
- Determination
- Hypothesising what will happen in an experiment
- Calculating the area of a triangle

Is it all of them, or just some of them? Why?

Cards on the table: I wouldn't classify everything here as a 'skill'. For me, *motivation*, *determination* and *resilience* are better thought of as **attributes** (behavioural characteristics) because they don't fit the conceptualisation that **skills are knowledge in action**.[75] This isn't to say attributes are any less important than skills, or that schools shouldn't play an important role in developing students' attributes. It's just to make the point that, as we discussed in Part 1, attributes aren't quite the same as skills.

Categories of skill

Building on this, while I would classify *most* of the options as 'skills', I would want to be able to use **different categories** (much like 'animals' can be categorised as 'vertebrates', 'mammals', and so on). The reason is because of the significant differences between many of the options, such as 'calculating the area of a triangle' and 'critical-thinking', relating to their **specificity**. Comparing 'calculating the area of a triangle' and 'critical-thinking' is a bit like comparing pears and a fruit bowl – while they both relate to fruit, the specific nature of one (pears) makes this significantly different from the non-specific other (the fruit bowl).

75 We discussed attributes in some detail in Part 1.

Accepting this, I would suggest the following categorisation:[76]

Category 1	Category 2	Category 3
Using full stops in a sentence Calculating the area of a triangle	Summarising the main idea of a message Hypothesising what will happen in an experiment	Critical-thinking Problem-solving Creativity Communication Collaboration

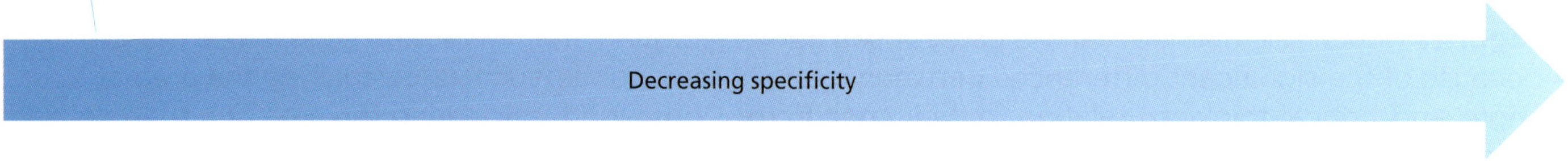

The reason it can be useful to categorise skills in this way relates to **how we teach skills** and their **transferability**. The best way to teach Category 1 skills isn't the same as Category 2 or 3. Nor are Category 1, 2 and 3 skills equally transferable. These are the themes to which we will now turn our attention.

What do we mean by 'transferable skills'?

Starting with the theme of transferability, take a moment to consider the question: **What do you understand by the term 'transferable skills'?**

76 If you think that 'motivation', 'determination' and 'resilience' should be classified as skills (rather than attributes), I would suggest these belong in Category 3.

To most people, a 'transferable skill' is one that, **once taught, can be used in different subjects and life beyond school**. This is the meaning we shall use moving forward.

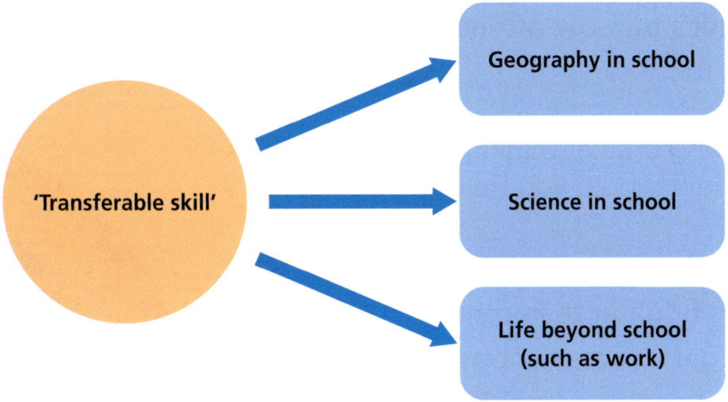

Which skills are transferable?

Accepting the definition above, take a moment to consider the following multiple-choice question:

Which of the following skills would you categorise as a 'transferable skill'?

A Critical-thinking
B Summarising the main idea
C Calculating the area of a triangle

In my experience, most people would choose A and / or B (which is fine, because sometimes there can be more than one correct answer in a multiple-choice question). But are they right?

Let's explore this by considering each option in some detail.

Option A: Critical-thinking

To help consider option A, let's turn our attention to rainbows.

Rainbows

If someone asked the following critical-thinking questions about rainbows, how confident would you be that you could answer each one correctly?

1. What causes rainbows?
2. Why are some rainbows brighter than others?
3. Why do we sometimes get double rainbows?
4. Are we more likely to get a rainbow on a hot day than a cold day, or does this not make any difference?

Thinking requires knowledge

Your ability to think critically about each question depends on **how much knowledge** you have stored in long-term memory about the topic at hand (in this case, that would include the electromagnetic spectrum, wavelengths and refraction). You draw on this knowledge both automatically and with deliberate effort, **applying it as skill** (in this case, to answer each question correctly).

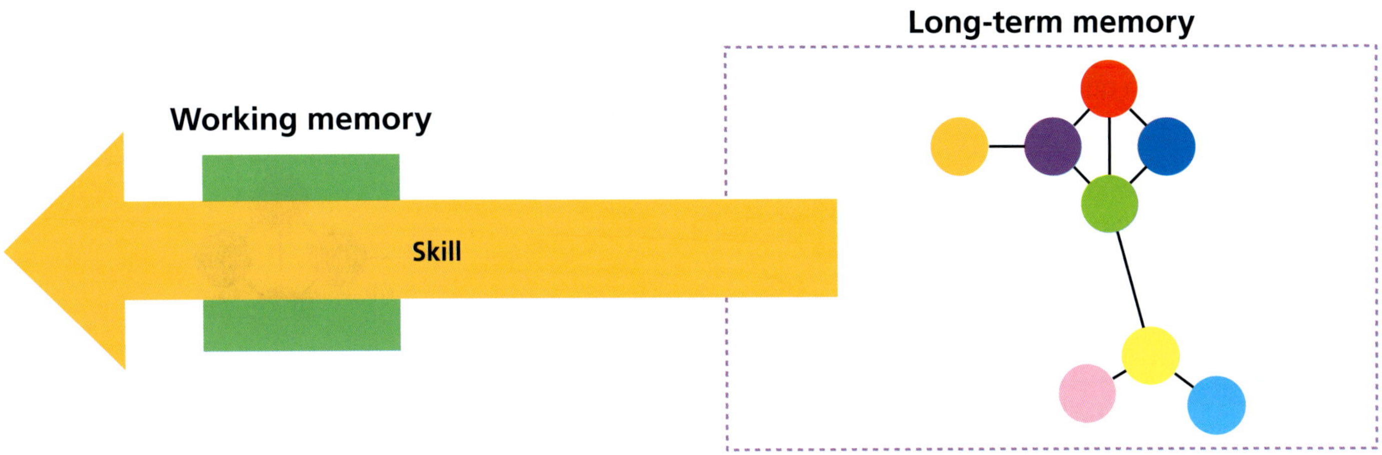

Now, let's turn our attention to earthquakes.

Earthquakes

If someone asked the following critical-thinking questions about earthquakes, how confident would you be that you could answer each one correctly?

1 What causes earthquakes?
2 Why are some earthquakes more severe than others?
3 Why do some earthquakes last longer than others?
4 Is an earthquake more likely to happen in a country nearer or further away from the equator, or does it not make any difference?

Again, your ability to think critically will depend on the **knowledge you have stored in long-term memory** about the subject at hand. The broader and deeper your subject knowledge, the better your critical-thinking about each question is likely to be.

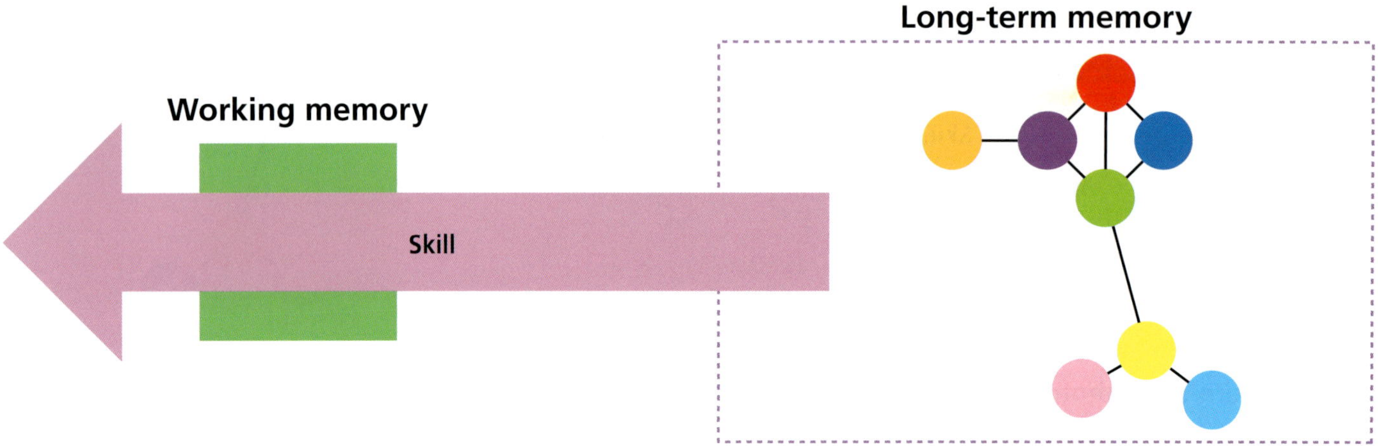

Now, ask yourself: Does the ability to think critically about rainbows help you to think critically about earthquakes (and vice versa)?

The answer should be 'no'. Thinking critically about different things requires different knowledge. What this means is that, contrary to popular belief, **critical-thinking isn't a transferable skill**.

Doug Lemov captures this neatly:

> You can think deeply only about things you know something about – the more you know, the more deeply and creatively.[77]

---

77 Lemov, D. (2021) *Teach Like a Champion 3.0*

Critical-thinking isn't even a skill

Taking this a step further, some prominent educationalists argue that the non-specific nature of critical-thinking (and other Category 3 skills) means this isn't really a 'skill' at all. For example, Dylan Wiliam:

> Critical thinking is not a skill. It is a collection of many skills.[78]

And E.D. Hirsch:

> 'Critical thinking' as it is typically discussed is a misguided educational fad... What people call critical thinking is either a class of very specific reasoning skills, or the formation of [knowledge] expertise in a field.[79]

Umbrella terms

I agree. 'Critical-thinking', 'problem-solving', 'creativity', 'communication' and 'collaboration' (and anything else that belongs in Category 3) would be better thought of as broad **umbrella terms** for more specific sets of skills that sit under these labels.

Returning to our multiple-choice question, because it isn't transferable and because it's not even really a skill, we should rule out option A.

Which of the following skills would you categorise as a 'transferable skill'?

~~A Critical-thinking~~
B Summarising the main idea
C Calculating the area of a triangle

78 Wiliam, D. (2018) *Creating the Schools Our Children Need*
79 Hirsch, E.D. (2016) *Why Knowledge Matters*

Option B: Summarising the main idea

Having concluded that, contrary to popular belief, 'critical-thinking' isn't a transferable skill, let's turn our attention to option B of the multiple-choice question: 'Summarising the main idea'. Is this a transferable skill?

A 'summarising the main idea' activity

To explore this, take a moment to read the following passage and then ask yourself: **On a scale of 1–10, how confident am I that I could summarise the main idea?**

Passage A

No matter how hard you try, you will never be able to grasp just how tiny, how spatially unassuming, is a proton. It is just way too small. A proton is an infinitesimal part of an atom, which is itself of course an insubstantial thing. Protons are so small that a little dib of ink like the dot on this i can hold something in the region of 500,000,000,000 of them, rather more than the number of seconds contained in half a million years. So protons are exceedingly microscopic, to say the very least. Now imagine, if you can (and of course you can't), shrinking one of those protons down to a billionth of its normal size into a space so small that it would make a proton look enormous. Now pack into that tiny, tiny space about an ounce of matter. Excellent. You are ready to start a universe.[80]

80 Bryson, B. (2025) *A Short History of Nearly Everything 2.0*

Now, repeat this exercise with a different passage:

Passage B

The biosynthesis of L-ascorbic acid (vitamin C) is not well understood in plants. The ozone-sensitive Arabidopsis thaliana mutant vitamin c-1 (vtc1; formerly known as soz1) is deficient in ascorbic acid, accumulating approximately 30% of wild-type levels. This deficiency could result from elevated catabolism or decreased biosynthesis. No differences that could account for the deficiency were found in the activities of enzymes that catalyse the oxidation or reduction of ascorbic acid.[81]

How do your scores compare?

Most people will score higher for passage A than B. The reason is that they **know more** about passage A. This means they **understand more** about the passage, so they can summarise it better. If the pre-requisite subject knowledge isn't stored in long-term memory, people will find it difficult (or impossible) to understand what they are reading and so will find it difficult (or impossible) to summarise the main idea.[82] This is why Daniel Willingham has suggested that reading tests are really knowledge tests in disguise.[83] It is also why Dylan Wiliam has made the following point about reading comprehension:

> ... the difficulties children have making progress in reading [usually] stem not from a lack of reading skill but from a **lack of background knowledge** about what is being described in the text.[84]

---

81 Conklin, P.L., Pallanca, R.L. and Smirnoff, N. (1997) 'L-ascorbic acid metabolism in the ascorbate-deficient arabidopsis mutant vtc1'
82 https://teachlikeachampion.org/blog/the-science-of-reading-its-about-knowledge-not-transferable-skills (Accessed: 26 March 2026)
83 Willingham, D.T. (2015) *Raising Kids Who Read*
84 Wiliam, D. (2018) *Creating the Schools Our Children Need*

While students can - and should - be taught generic strategies that can help them to summarise the main idea (such as homing in on key words and phrases; identifying and filtering out any non-essential information; and editing their answer to be as concise as possible, removing words and phrases that are superfluous), they will be able to put these into action *only* if they **also** have subject knowledge relating to what they are reading. In *Why Knowledge Matters*, E.D. Hirsch makes this point:

> We know that the skill of reading comprehension in any given case depends more on relevant knowledge than on formal strategies. Once briefly learned, the strategies will take care of themselves.[85]

Subject knowledge matters most

Building on this, a key point to emphasise is that the role generic 'summarising the main idea' strategies and subject knowledge play in helping students summarise the main idea isn't an equal one - **subject knowledge matters most**.[86]

To appreciate this, imagine two students, Marnie and Max, who are being asked to summarise the main idea of a passage on climate change. Marnie has been taught lots about climate change but little about how to summarise the main idea. Max is the opposite, having been taught very little about climate change but a lot about how to summarise the main idea. Who does better?

Almost certainly, it is Marnie.[87] While helpful, generic 'summarising the main idea' strategies will only get Max so far. **Knowledge of the subject at hand** is the key factor in determining success.

---

85 Hirsch, E.D. (2016) *Why Knowledge Matters*
86 The same principle applies to other Category 2 skills, such as hypothesising what will happen in an experiment.
87 This example is adapted from research discussed in Willingham, D.T. (2010) *Why Don't Students Like School?*

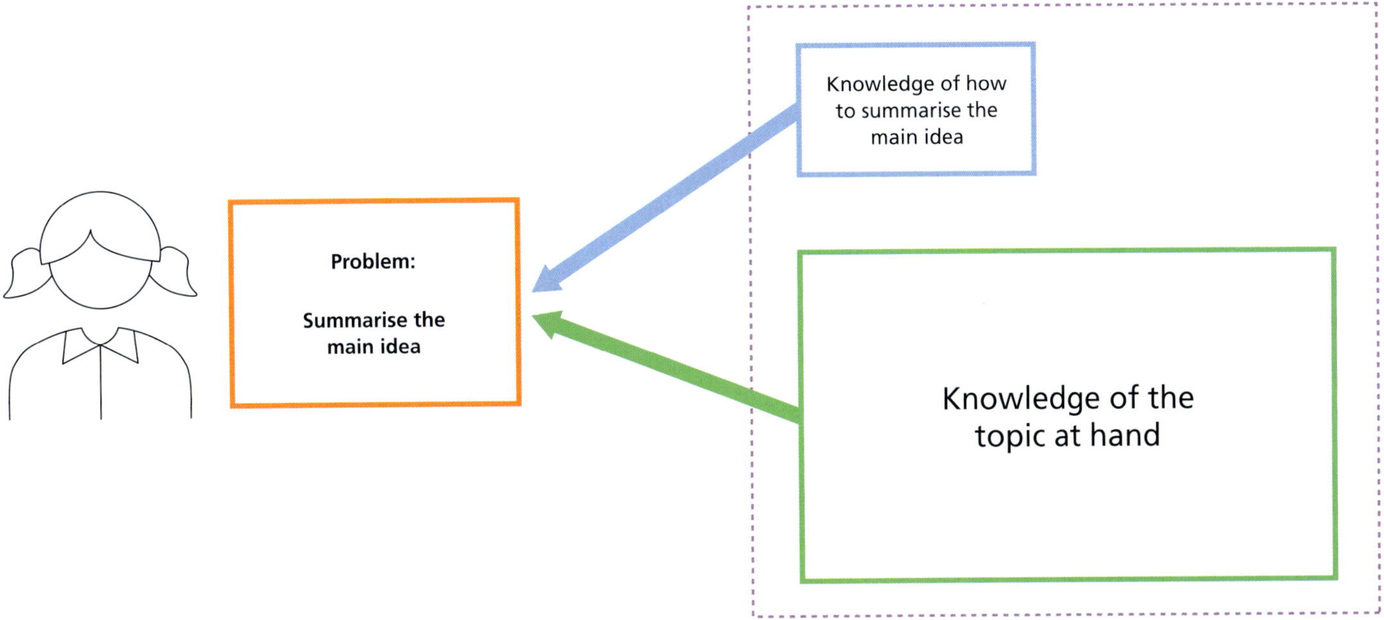

The thinking-skills paradox

It is perfectly possible that Marnie would have been able to summarise the main idea of the passage without having been taught anything about how to summarise the main idea, which brings us to the **thinking-skills paradox**:[88] the best way to teach thinking skills usually isn't to focus on them directly.[89]

---

88 By 'thinking skills', we mean those in Categories 2 and 3.
89 Wiliam, D. (2018) *Creating the Schools Our Children Need*

Giving students lots of practice in summarising the main idea won't help them to become better at summarising the main idea of different passages. Summarising the main idea of anything requires understanding, and the key to developing understanding is **subject knowledge** – which is what teaching should focus on.

Accepting this, anyone involved in developing or reviewing a curriculum should call out content statements that look anything like the following example:

> To show my understanding, I can comment, with evidence, on the content and form of short and extended texts, and respond to literal, inferential and evaluative questions and other types of close-reading tasks.[90]

Putting to one side the fact such statements are incredibly difficult to understand in themselves, it's hard to accept what value they have for teachers. Just because students can respond to literal, inferential or evaluative questions relating to one text (such as *The Lion, The Witch and The Wardrobe*), it doesn't mean they will be able to do the same with another, especially if this is more challenging (such as *Great Expectations*). Therefore, what is the point of including statements like this in curriculum documentation?

Developing reading comprehension

If we want students to develop reading comprehension, including with increasingly challenging texts, the best way to do this is to:

1. teach students a broad, deep body of knowledge within subjects that they can use to think with
2. ensure there are frequent opportunities for students to read, discuss and write about increasingly challenging texts in as many subjects as possible.[91, 92]

---

90 https://auth.education.gov.scot/media/wpsnskgv/all-experiencesoutcomes18.pdf (Accessed: 26 March 2026)
91 Robertson, B. (2021) *The Teaching Delusion 2*
92 Exceptions to this rule would be subjects such as maths and home economics, where this might become tokenistic.

With all of this in mind and returning to our multiple-choice question, we should rule out option B as well.

Which of the following skills would you categorise as a 'transferable skill'?

~~A Critical-thinking~~
~~B Summarising the main idea~~
C Calculating the area of a triangle

Option C: Calculating the area of a triangle

Having concluded that 'summarising the main idea' and 'critical-thinking' aren't transferable skills (and, by extension, the other Category 2 and 3 skills we highlighted earlier), let's turn our attention to option C of our multiple-choice question: Is 'calculating the area of a triangle' a transferable skill?

'Calculating the area of a triangle' problems

To explore this, imagine students have been taught how to calculate the area of the following triangles in maths:

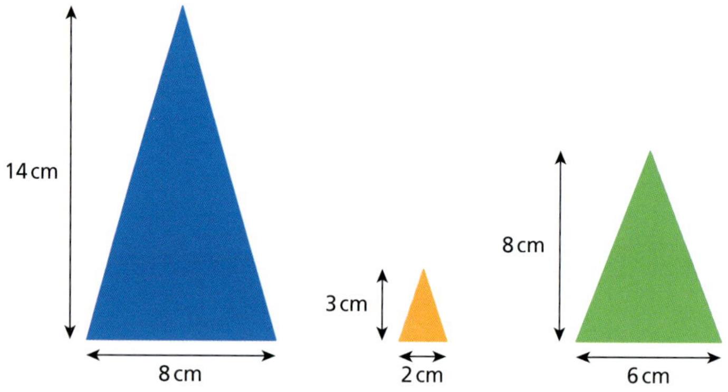

If shown the following triangle, should they be able to calculate its area?

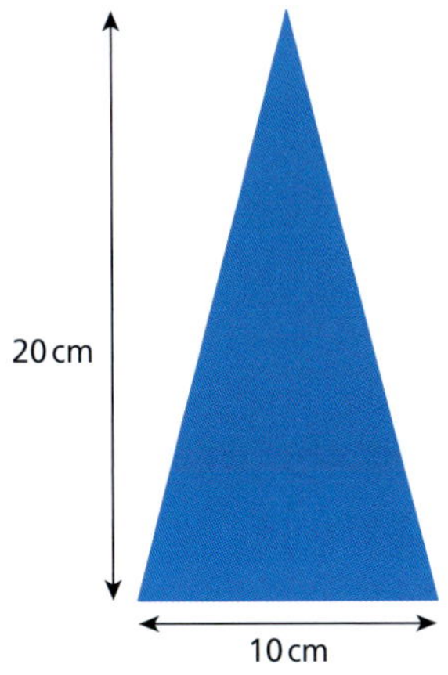

The answer is (probably) yes. Students should be able to apply knowledge they have been taught previously to solve an unfamiliar problem. The skill is **transferable within the knowledge domain** of calculating triangles.

More than this – and this is a key point – beyond being able to apply the skill in maths, students should be able to apply this skill to **any situation** that requires it.[93] That includes in science, geography, technologies and the world beyond school. This isn't true for 'summarising the main idea' or 'critical-thinking'.

93 The caveat being that the unfamiliar problem isn't significantly different, requiring additional knowledge that students might not have.

If our definition of a 'transferable skill' is one that, **once taught, can be used in different subjects and life beyond school**, then 'calculating the area of a triangle' (and other Category A skills) fits this definition. For that reason, returning to our multiple-choice question, the answer is C:

Which of the following skills would you categorise as a 'transferable skill'?

~~**A Critical thinking**~~
~~**B Summarising the main idea**~~
C Calculating the area of a triangle

Specificity and subject knowledge determine transferability

All of this brings us to the important conclusion that the transferability of any skill really depends on two factors:

1 Specificity

2 The link to subject knowledge.

'Calculating the area of a triangle' is a **specific skill** that is **intrinsically linked to subject knowledge**, making it transferable to different situations requiring this skill, such as in maths, science, geography, and so on.

'Summarising the main idea' is a **non-specific skill** that can be transferred to new situations **only if** it is accompanied with relevant subject knowledge. Effectively, subject knowledge acts as a bridge between **knowing how to do something in a generic way** and **actually being able to do this** in specific situations:

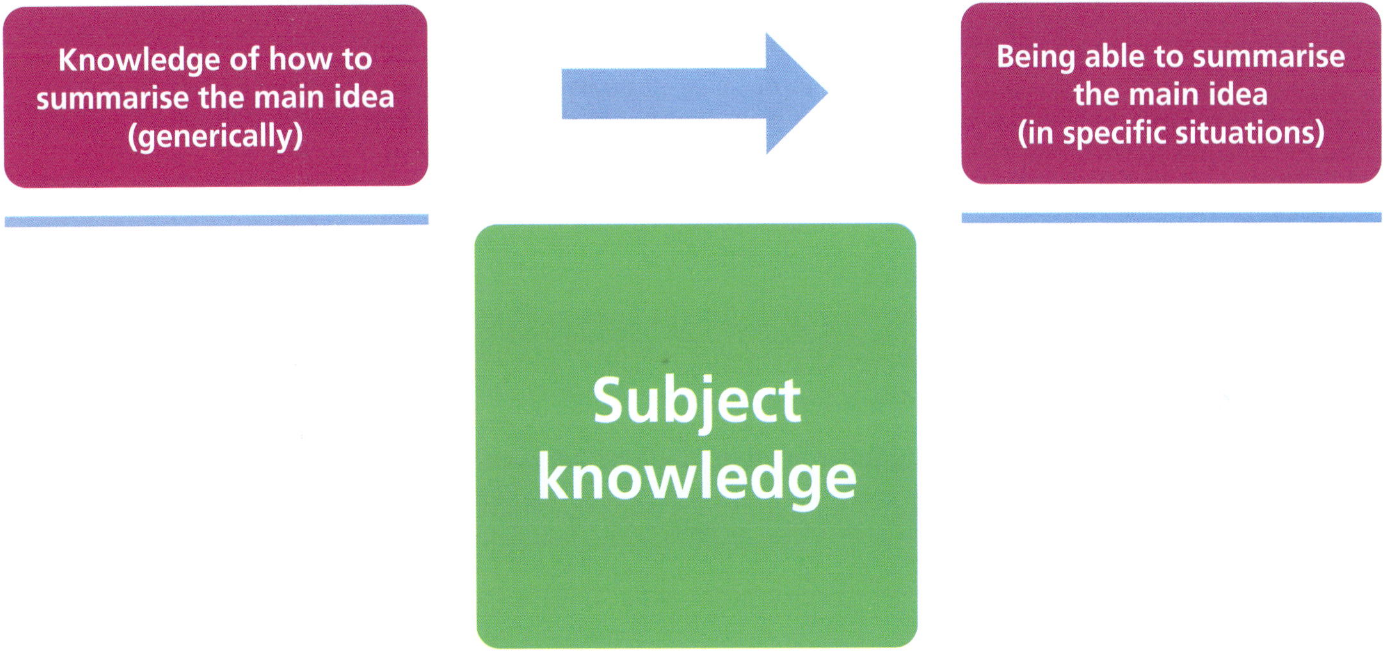

This conclusion underpins an anecdote that I shared in *The Teaching Delusion 2* and that I think is worth re-sharing here as an end to this section:

> I was once interviewed for a job and as part of the interview I was asked a problem-solving question relating to school budgets. At the time, what I knew about managing school budgets could have been written on the back of a £5 note, using very big writing. The interviewer could see I was struggling. To try to help, he asked if I had a 'problem-solving strategy' that I could use to help

me. I thought about this for a moment. Nothing. Knowing that I had to say something, I told him that if I didn't know how to solve a problem, I would probably do research to find an answer, or I would ask someone for help. I don't think this is what he was looking for – and I didn't get the job – but I stand by what I said. There is no such thing as a 'problem-solving strategy' that we can teach people so they can solve any problem they might encounter. **Whether or not you can solve a problem depends on the extent to which you have domain-specific knowledge relating to that problem.** You can think about a problem as hard as you like – if you don't have the domain-specific knowledge to help you solve it, you won't be able to.[94]

Focused reflection

- What are your key takeaways from this section?
- If you are a teacher or leader, are there any implications for your teaching or leadership?
- If you are a parent, what questions might you have for your child's school in relation to the points being made?

94 Robertson, B. (2021) *The Teaching Delusion 2*

Curriculum Concept 4: The best way to teach meta-skills is to focus on knowledge

Common pitfall: We try to teach generic 'meta-skills' in the absence of subject knowledge.

Meta-skills

Increasingly in education and wider employment, the term **meta-skills** is being used in place of 'transferable skills' (by which people generally mean critical-thinking, problem-solving, creativity, communication and collaboration).[95]

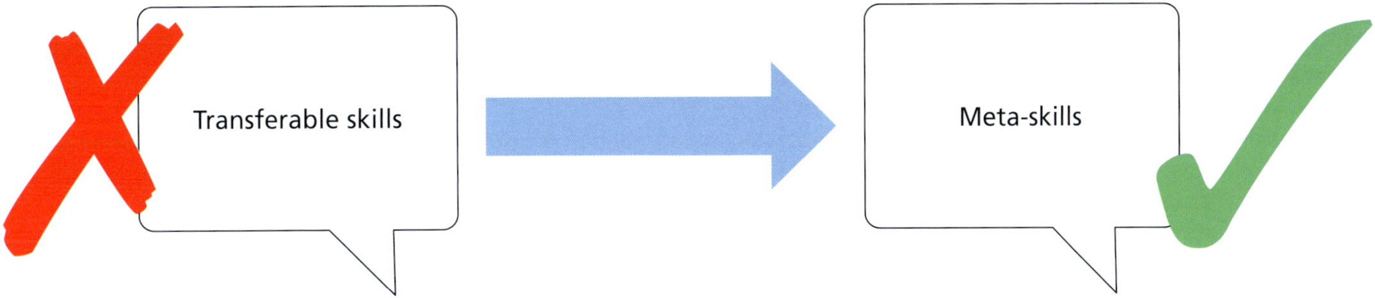

95 Wiliam, D. (2018) *Creating the Schools Our Children Need*

On the one hand, this is sensible for at least two reasons:

1. As we have discussed, many 'skills' that get labelled as 'transferable' aren't actually as transferable as we might like to believe.
2. The prefix *meta* means **alongside**. Because 'skills' such as critical-thinking **can be used only if there is supporting subject knowledge**, 'meta-skills' is a phrase that captures this better.

However, on the other hand, many issues persist. One is that, as we discussed in the previous sections, the things people generally refer to as meta-skills aren't really 'skills' - they are broad umbrella terms for more specific sets of skills that sit beneath the label. Another is that, ironically, the misunderstanding of transferability has transferred to the new terminology. One more issue is the belief that meta-skills can be taught in the absence of knowledge - which they can't.

Meta-skills progression frameworks

We can see these issues play out when schools try to use 'meta-skills progression frameworks' to support teaching and learning, such as the following example for critical-thinking:[96]

> ### Critical thinking
> **Critical thinking is the ability to process, analyse and evaluate information to solve problems, or understand a situation and make decisions in a variety of contexts.**
>
> The ability to solve complex problems can include:
>
> - **Deconstruction:** Breaking down a complex problem or system into smaller, more manageable parts before developing a new way of addressing the problem
> - **Logical thinking:** The ability to identify, analyse and evaluate situations, ideas and information in order to formulate responses to problems
> - **Judgement:** The act or process of forming an opinion after careful thought
> - **Computational thinking:** The ability to translate vast amounts of data into abstract concepts and to understand data-based reasoning

96 www.skillsdevelopmentscotland.co.uk/media/rbmj1kjm/meta-skills-progression-framework.pdf

Learners show critical-thinking at Early Level by:	Learners show critical-thinking at First Level by:	Learners show critical-thinking at Second Level by:	Learners show critical-thinking at Third / Fourth Level by:	Learners show critical-thinking in Senior Level by:
• working with a focus, asking and responding to questions to clarify what they are doing • making simple predictions and seeing possibilities • asking different types of questions • summarising and reflecting on their learning • using materials from their environment and coming up with their own ideas on how to solve problems.	• asking focused questions to clarify tasks and what needs to be done to plan and to set goals • beginning to test predictions and look for evidence • being systematic and working through the stages of a task • recognising the difference between why, what, where, when and how questions • explaining their methods and opinions when evaluating work, and beginning to justify their choices and actions • applying strategies to help solve problems in a variety of contexts including real life, learning and play.	• using different types of questions systematically and with purpose • making and testing predictions, examining evidence and making links between possible causes and effects • examining options when working through a task and weighing up the pros and cons of different approaches • explaining and justifying methods, opinions and conclusions while understanding more than one point of view • selecting the most appropriate strategy to solve a problem and complete a task.	• explaining processes, concepts or ideas confidently, and being able to explain links between possible causes and effects • identifying and raising issues, drawing conclusions and summarising their findings • examining the pros and cons of a decision, predicting likely consequences and evaluating the outcomes from a range of perspectives • identifying an appropriate strategy to solve complex problems in order to complete tasks.	• explaining complex processes or concepts with relevant supporting detail and evidence and can confidently justify their reasoning • presenting complex ideas or issues in an appropriate way to different audiences • posing questions about the reliability of evidence and the consequences for reaching conclusions • presenting relational opinions and conclusions based on a combination of their own and others' point of view • identifying and evaluating complex problem-solving strategies, demonstrating to others their process for reaching that conclusion in a logical way.

A usefulness mirage

As is so often the case with frameworks of this kind, while at first glance they might appear to be useful, closer scrutiny reveals a mirage.

Sticking with the example shown, there are at least three reasons why this is unlikely to be useful (and more likely to lead to problems):

1. The statements are **too vague and ambiguous** to have any realistic chance of developing a shared meaning. Different people are likely to interpret each statement differently, and some people won't understand what some of the statements mean at all (I put myself in the latter category).
2. Most statements in most categories could be lifted and put into any other category, which means **they don't really signpost progression**. For example, 'selecting the most appropriate strategy to solve a problem and complete a task' (Second Level) could apply as much to learning to build a sandcastle (Early Level) as to solving quantum mechanics calculations (Senior Level).

3 Even if the meaning of each statement was clear and there was real progression from level to level, for reasons we have previously discussed, most of the skills included **aren't transferable across knowledge domains**. Therefore, there is no point using a progression framework to map them out. A student might be able to 'explain processes, concepts or ideas confidently' in one aspect of biology (such as mitosis) but unable to do this in another (such as the Krebs' Cycle) or in different subjects, such as history and maths.

While we **do** want students to develop meta-skills, and I would argue this is an important goal of teaching, we shouldn't fall into the trap of believing 'meta-skills progression frameworks' will support this. If we take a step back and ask, 'Will frameworks of this kind help teachers teach and students learn?', the honest answer is almost certainly 'no'. More likely, they will tie everyone in knots trying to understand how to use them and consume time that could otherwise have been spent on more valuable activities.[97]

Moderation meetings

For example, over the last decade or more in Scotland, teachers have been asked to spend countless hours engaging in never-ending cycles of 'moderation meetings', whereby they come together with pieces of student work and try to determine where these fit in a progression framework. While the opportunity for professional dialogue among teachers is almost always a good thing, the word 'almost' is one to emphasise here. Teachers are being asked to work together to solve a Rubik's Cube in a pitch-black room. It should therefore come as no surprise that most teachers are screaming for a light to be turned on and to be given useful instructions about what they should actually be doing.

97 We will gloss over the fact similar meta-skills progression frameworks have been produced by organisations such as Skills Development Scotland for attributes such as 'integrity', 'adapting', 'initiative' and 'curiosity'. I think all the points that need to be made about the unhelpfulness of progression frameworks have been made already.

Teaching meta-skills

As we highlighted in Curriculum Concept 3, counterintuitively the best things to do to get good at something don't always look like the something we are trying to get good at.[98] We see this a lot in professional sport, with the drills being practised having little resemblance to the final performance – I'm yet to watch a professional football match that has cones spread down the middle of the pitch.

And so it is with meta-skills. While we **do** want students to develop these, the best way to help them usually isn't to focus on the meta-skills themselves. As Clare Sealy has eloquently written:

> Put simply, one does not learn how to think critically, or problem solve or be creative by being taught a curriculum that directly focuses on these things. While one can see how this might appear to be logical at first glance, when we dig deeper beyond what feels like it must be true, we find there is indisputable evidence, both scientific and in practice, that refutes this.[99]

Focus on subject knowledge and its application

The key to developing meta-skills is to **teach students subject knowledge** and to ensure they have regular **opportunities to apply this** in structured and unstructured ways.

---

98 Wiliam, D. (2018) *Creating the Schools Our Children Need*

99 Sealy, C. (2025) 'Knowledge And Skills: A Journey Not A Dichotomy' in *The value of a knowledge-rich curriculum: An essay collection* [online] Available at: www.civitas.org.uk/publications/knowledge-rich-curriculum (Accessed: 26 March 2026)

For example, students might be taught about renewable and non-renewable energy sources and asked to:

- answer a set of questions to check understanding (structured application of subject knowledge)
- discuss the advantages and disadvantages of both (unstructured application of subject knowledge)
- ask their own questions about both (unstructured application of subject knowledge).

The more subject knowledge students have, the better their answers, discussions and own questions are likely to be. As we have said previously: **knowledge is thinking fuel**.

Critical-thinking and problem-solving

Taking critical-thinking and problem-solving as specific examples, the best way to teach these in subjects is through a **focus on subject-specific knowledge and its application**. Maths should teach critical-thinking and problem-solving in maths, history should teach critical-thinking and problem-solving in history, and so on. Being able to think critically and solve problems in maths does not mean you can do the same in history or any other subject.

In teaching such 'skills', teachers should keep returning to three fundamental questions:

1. What do I want students to think critically and solve problems *about*?
2. What knowledge do students need to be taught to *think with*?
3. What opportunities can I create for students to *use this knowledge*?

Teaching creativity

Taking 'creativity' as a further example, imagine students are set one or more of the following 'creativity tasks':

- Write about a new dinosaur that has just been discovered.
- Design a new emoji.
- Compose a new piece of music.

The starting point in all tasks will be students' **knowledge of the subject at hand**.

For example, to write about a new dinosaur, students will first need to consider what they already know about dinosaurs. The more they know, the more likely they will produce something that is both new and 'valuable'.[100]

Homing in on this latter point, students who don't know much about dinosaurs are more likely to write about dinosaurs that can breathe fire and fly to the moon than students who know more and realise such things go beyond the limits of what dinosaurs would ever realistically be able to do. While I am sure there will be some people who say, 'What's wrong with that – they're being creative', I would counter that creativity doesn't mean 'anything goes'. Creativity in a **valuable** sense means **innovation within parameters**. Breathing fire and flying to the moon are examples of students going far beyond the parameters that most people would likely agree are sensible and reasonable. Dylan Wiliam offers another strong example:

> Blowing through the wrong end of a trumpet is not creative.[101]

As with other meta-skills, the best way to teach creativity is to **teach students a broad, deep body of knowledge** that they can draw upon and apply as skill (rather than build 'creativity lessons' into the school curriculum, like those that ask students to come up with 100 creative uses for a paperclip). David Bowie could be creative in his song-writing because he knew a lot about music, history and literature (and a lot more besides). Knowing more helped him to be more creative. And so it is in any field or subject in school. The more students know about things and how to do things (declarative and procedural knowledge), the more creative they are likely to be. They have a richer **knowledge palate** to draw upon and mix.

---

100 As discussed in more detail in: Badger, C. and Firth, J. (2025) *Creativity for Teachers*

101 Wiliam, D. (2025) 'Knowledge-Rich Curricula: A Key Driver Of Equity In Education' in *The value of a knowledge-rich curriculum: An essay collection* [online] Available at: www.civitas.org.uk/publications/knowledge-rich-curriculum (Accessed: 26 March 2026)

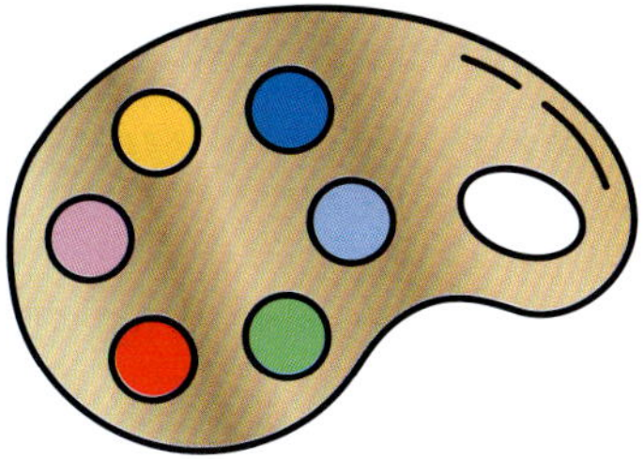

Focused reflection

- What are your key takeaways from this section?
- If you are a teacher or leader, are there any implications for your teaching or leadership?
- If you are a parent, what questions might you have for your child's school in relation to the points being made?

Curriculum Concept 5: When developing your curriculum, start with the big picture and work your way in

Common pitfall: A lack of clarity about the specific knowledge and skills we want students to learn, and the specific experiences we want them to have.

What should we include in our curriculum?

Towards the start of this book, I asked you to consider the quality of the curriculum in your team or school, suggesting this is difficult (or impossible) to evaluate if you don't have clarity about the specific **knowledge** and **skills** you want students to learn, and the specific **experiences** you want them to have. *Curriculum* means 'content' so if content isn't clear, you don't really have a curriculum.

Accepting this, logical questions to ask ourselves are:

- **What** knowledge and skills should students be learning?
- **What** experiences should students be having?

In other words: **What should we include in our curriculum?**

Over the course of Curriculum Concepts 5 and 6, this is the question we are going to explore. The overarching steer is: **Start with the big picture and work your way in**. If we don't know where we're going, we won't know how to get there.[102]

---

102 Wiliam, D. (2018) *Creating the Schools Our Children Need*

Levels of organisation

To help us decide where we are going and how to get there, it can be helpful to think of the curriculum in four hierarchical levels:

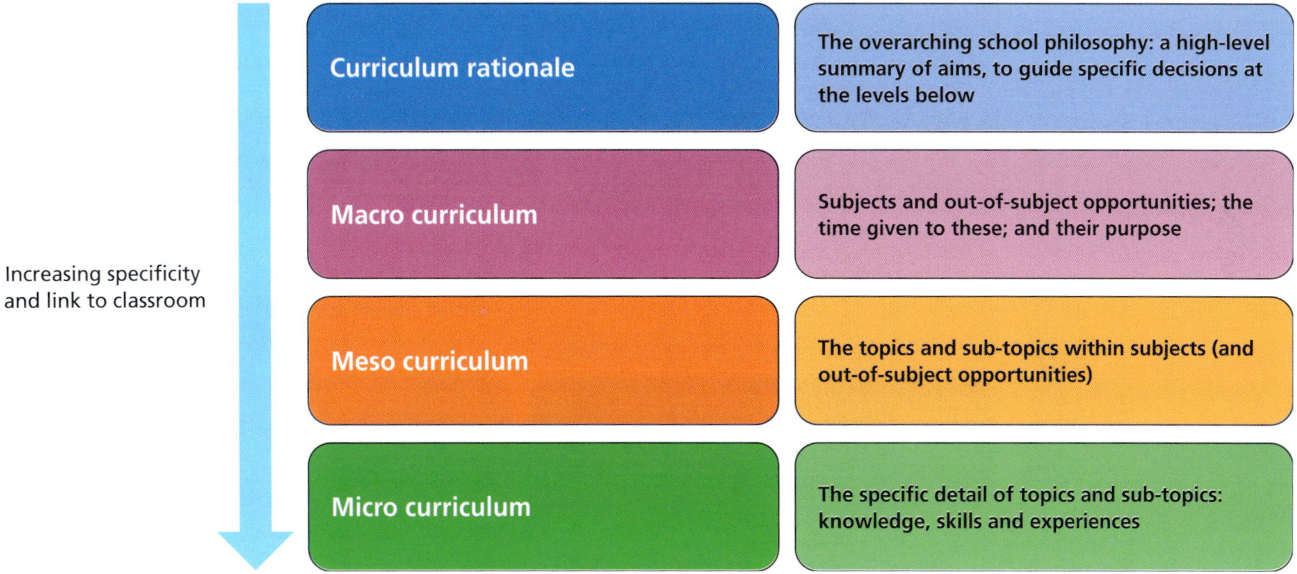

Let's take time to unpack each level.

Curriculum rationale

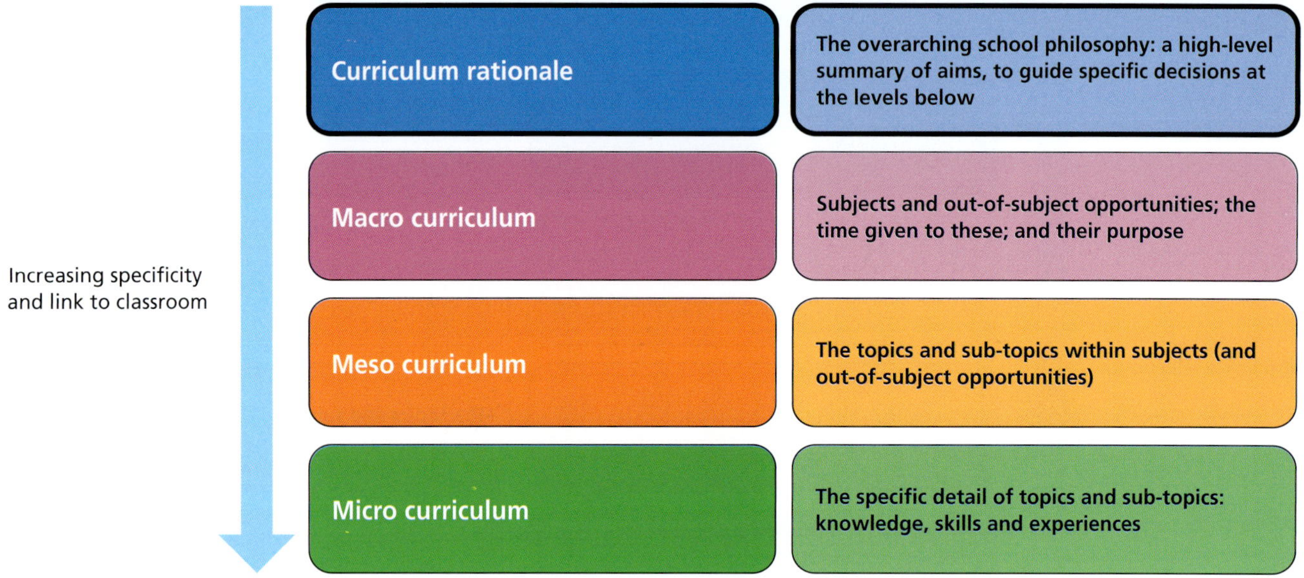

The first level of curriculum organisation is the **curriculum rationale** for a school.

By this, we mean the overarching philosophy of what the curriculum is trying to achieve. In other words: **the purpose of our school curriculum**. This is the starting point from which more specific decisions can be made at the levels below.[103] As we shall go on to discuss, a clear curriculum rationale can help bring cohesion to the school curriculum as a whole.[104]

For example, a school's curriculum rationale might look as follows:[105]

The purpose of our school curriculum is to give all students:

- knowledge that they can use to **think critically**, **solve problems** and **be creative** in a wide range of contexts
- knowledge and skills that should be **useful in the wider world**
- knowledge we hope they will find **interesting**
- knowledge and skills that will help them **achieve the qualifications** they are aiming for
- experiences that are **enriching** and that **develop attributes**, reflecting our school values.

103 van den Akker, J. (2003) *Curriculum Perspectives*
104 Myatt, M. (2018) *The Curriculum*
105 Note: this should be viewed as an example, not a definitive version.

What you include matters

The detail of a school's curriculum rationale is important because it **signposts** the ultimate aims of learning in subjects and out-of-subject opportunities. This can help teachers and leaders make decisions about what to include in the curriculum at the macro, meso and micro levels. For example, if a school's curriculum rationale includes 'critical-thinking', 'problem-solving' and 'creativity', this makes it clear that there should be a focus on such things in subjects over periods of time (though not necessarily in every lesson).

'Interesting' and 'useful'

If it includes the statement 'Knowledge we hope [students] will find **interesting**' (as in the earlier example), this gives a clear steer to teachers and leaders that they have permission to go beyond the concept of 'useful' when making decisions about what to include in the curriculum. If 'useful' is included but 'interesting' isn't, we risk all kinds of potentially interesting and valuable knowledge falling to the cutting-room floor. For example:

- knowledge of galaxies – **not useful**
- knowledge of Dickens – **not useful**
- knowledge of tidal waves – **not useful**.

While we **do** want the curriculum to be useful, an overemphasis on 'useful' can be reductive as a content driver. 'Interesting' should be seen as important a content driver as 'useful' and a key part of a teacher's job is to help make content interesting, particularly that which students might be less inclined to naturally find interesting. Pedagogically, a good way to do that is to ask questions and pose problems about it. For example, when teaching students about weight and mass in science, a teacher might pose the question: If we drop a rock into a bucket of water on the moon, will it sink as it would on Earth?

'Real life' can help, but it's not essential

With 'interesting' in mind, it is often suggested that the best way to do this is to link content to 'real life', by which is usually meant the things students might be interested in or can relate to already. However, while this certainly can help, we won't be able to do it all the time, and we shouldn't try to. Some learning is abstract and impossible to link to 'real life', but that doesn't mean we can't make it interesting through the way it is taught. Plus, a key purpose of school should be to develop students' knowledge and understanding **far beyond** that of their 'real lives'. Carl Hendrick captures this idea nicely:

> Possibly the greatest thing a teacher can do is introduce students to wonderous worlds beyond the limited borders of their own experience, to allow them to see the previously unseen and to make new and enriching connections that were hitherto unavailable to them.[106]

106 Hendrick, C. (2017) [online] Available at: www.tes.com/magazine/archive/ken-robinson-teacher-basher-schools-must-stop-listening-his-panglossian-ideas (Accessed: 26 March 2026)

Macro curriculum

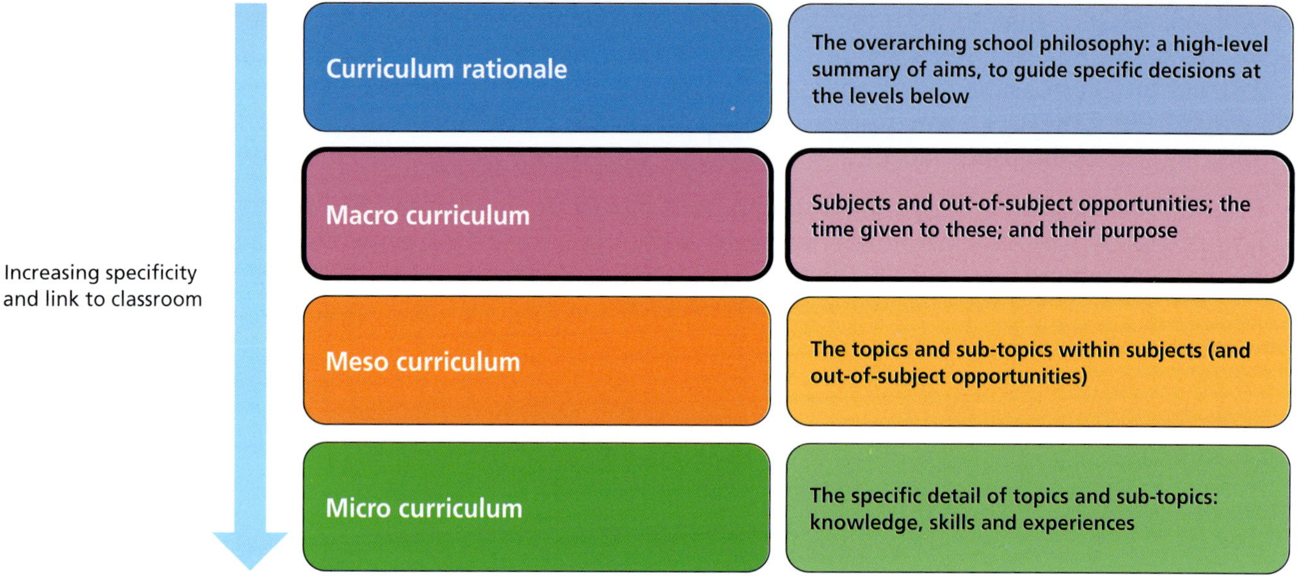

The second level of curriculum organisation is the **macro curriculum**.

By this, we mean the **subjects and out-of-subject opportunities** available to students,[107] the **time** we allocate to these (the timetable) and their **purpose**.

---

107 By 'subjects', we mean things like English, maths, science, history, art and PE; by 'out-of-subject opportunities', we mean things like clubs, sports and school shows.

Purpose steers content

While most leaders have a good handle on the subjects and out-of-subject opportunities available to students, including the time given to these, they don't always have the same handle on **purpose**. This is an issue, because **purpose steers content**.

For example, if we are clear that one of the purposes of music as a subject in the curriculum is 'to develop cultural literacy', this gives the steer that content should include components such as the history of music and works of specific artists. If this purpose isn't clear, there may or may not be a focus on such components in teaching.

Purpose can also influence pedagogy

A clear subject purpose can also influence some of the pedagogical decisions teachers make about how to teach a subject. For example:

- If one of the purposes of history is 'to develop students' literacy', this helps steer teachers towards pedagogies that emphasise reading, writing and discussion.
- If the purpose of science includes 'to learn to make predictions and generalisations' and 'to discuss contemporary scientific issues', teachers are given the steer that these are things students should be expected to do with their learning over periods of time (though not necessarily in every lesson).
- If a purpose of the school show is to help develop teamwork, teachers are more likely to ensure there are opportunities for students to work together, rather than just individually.

Meso curriculum

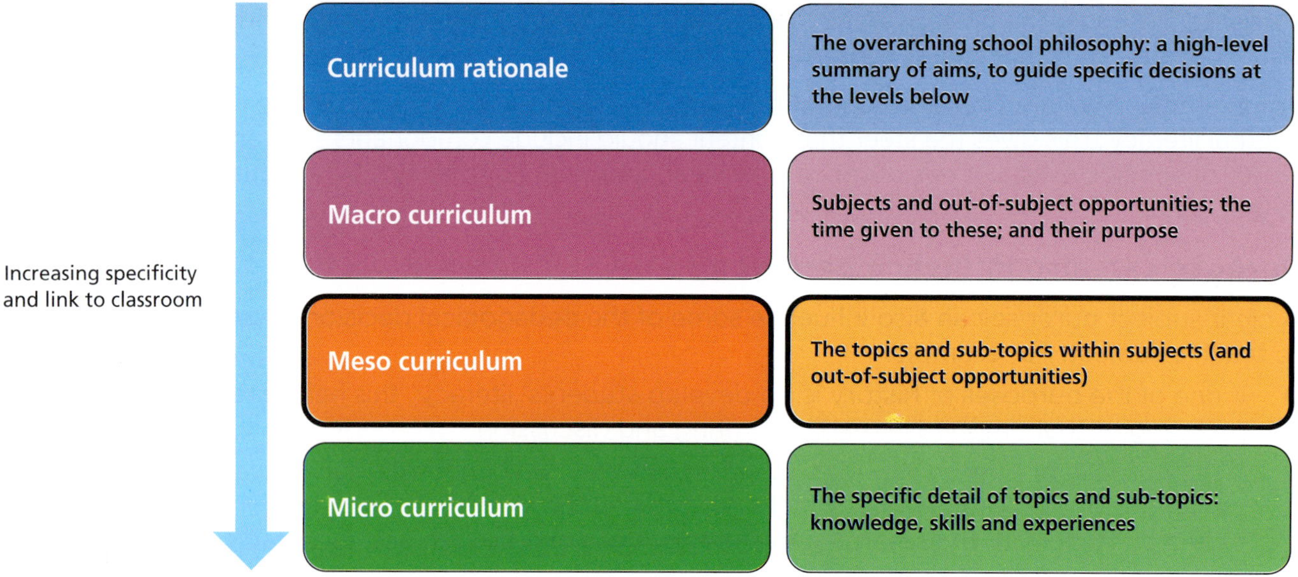

The third level of curriculum organisation is the **meso curriculum**.

By this, we mean the **topics** and **sub-topics** used to organise learning within subjects (and out-of-subject opportunities). For example:

Subject	**Art**	**English**	**Geography**	**Science**	**History**
Topic	Elements of art	Writing	The Earth	Chemical changes	Democracy
Sub-topics	• Line • Colour • Shape • Texture	• Narrative writing • Informative writing • Persuasive writing	• Geographical features of the Earth's surface • What's inside the Earth?	• Rates of reaction • Acids and alkalis	• Ancient Greek democracy • Democracy in the UK • Democracy in the USA

A thematic content organiser

Effectively, the meso curriculum is a **thematic content organiser**. This can be useful for anyone who wants to get a broad overview about what is being taught in subjects or across a school, without the need to go into the specific detail. This might include teachers, senior leaders and parents.

For example, a geography teacher might want to know if and when the science department is teaching content relating to their subject, such as the water cycle. A clear meso curriculum helps them find this out and to get into conversations with teachers from other subject areas. It might also influence their decisions about content to include or remove in their subject area (because it is or isn't being taught in another subject), or the best time to teach particular topics.

Pedagogical advice

At the meso curriculum level, it can be useful to share overarching pedagogical advice for teachers about how content should be taught (another example of curriculum overlapping with pedagogy). This might include signposting to previously taught content. For example, in art:

Lessons should illustrate important elements of making and appreciating art, and emphasise important artists, works of art and artistic concepts. When appropriate, topics may be linked to topics in other subjects. Examples given in curriculum documentation are not intended to be comprehensive. Teachers are encouraged to build upon the core content and expose students to a wide range of art and artists. In studying works of art, and in creating their own art, students should review, develop and apply concepts introduced in previous years, such as line, shape, form, space, texture, colour, light, design and symmetry.[108]

Link to formal assessment

At the meso curriculum level, it can also be useful to give details of any formal assessment that might take place towards the end of a topic (see Appendix 2 for a deeper exploration of this theme). For example, curriculum documentation might include statements such as:

- At the end of this topic, students' learning will be assessed via a 40-minute end-of-topic test, comprising multiple-choice and short-response questions.
- Learning from this topic will be assessed via an extended piece of writing [detail as follows...].

108 Adapted from: www.coreknowledge.org/wp-content/uploads/2016/09/CKFSequence_Rev.pdf

Micro curriculum

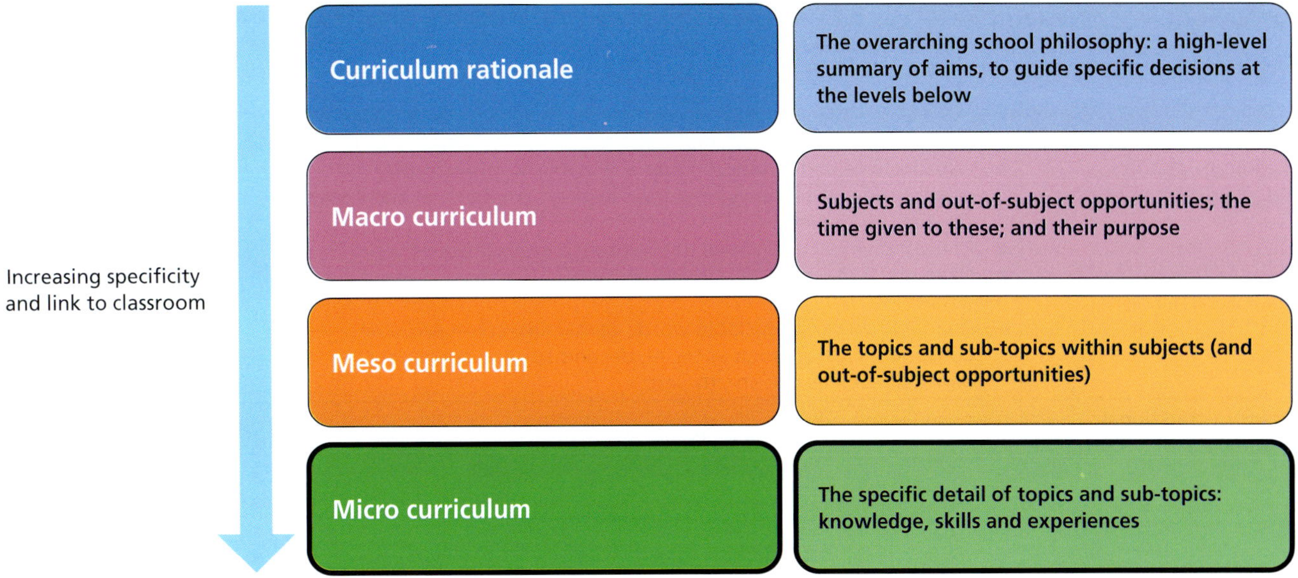

The fourth level of curriculum organisation is the **micro curriculum**.

By this, we mean the **specific knowledge and skills** we want all students to learn within topics and sub-topics, and the **specific experiences** we want all students to have. This is the purest level of the curriculum and the most important.

Programmes of Teaching and Learning

Programmes of Teaching and Learning can be used to set out and share the detail of a school's micro curriculum.[109] For example: [110]

English:[111]

Topic / sub-topic	Specific knowledge and skills	Specific experiences
Reading – phonics: decoding and encoding	• Demonstrate understanding that a systematic, predictable relationship exists between written letters (graphemes) and spoken sounds (phonemes). • Blend individual phonemes to pronounce printed words. • Read and write any CVC (consonant-vowel-consonant) word, e.g. sit or cat. • Read and write one-syllable words containing common initial consonant clusters such as tr-, fl-, dr- and sp- and consonant digraphs such as ch-, sh-, th-, etc.	
Poetry – traditional poems		Hearing and saying: • Diddle, Diddle, Dumpling • Georgie Porgie • Hey Diddle Diddle • Hickory, Dickory, Dock • Hot Cross Buns • Humpty Dumpty

109 To help parents understand what students should be learning, schools might decide to share Programmes of Teaching and Learning with parents, for example via the school website.

110 Some examples include *both* 'Specific knowledge and skills' and 'Specific experiences', while others only include one or the other. The approach taken will likely vary, depending on the topics and sub-topics being taught.

111 Adapted from: www.coreknowledge.org/wp-content/uploads/2016/09/CKFSequence_Rev.pdf

Maths:[112]

Topic / sub-topic	Specific knowledge and skills
Operations on whole numbers	• Solve multiplication and division problems working with whole numbers, using efficient written and mental methods, e.g. $94 \times 7 = 100 \times 7 - 6 \times 7$ • Multiply whole numbers by 2-digit numbers, e.g. $47 \times 12 = 47 \times 4 \times 3$ • Divide whole numbers by a single digit, e.g. $42 \div 6$

Science:[113]

Topic / sub-topic	Specific knowledge and skills	Specific experiences
Introduction to electricity	• Static electricity • Basic parts of simple electric circuits (e.g. batteries, wire, bulb or buzzer, switch) • Conductive and nonconductive materials • Safety rules for electricity (e.g. never put your finger, or anything metallic, in an electrical outlet; never touch a switch or electrical appliance when your hands are wet or when you're in the bathtub; never put your finger in a lamp socket; etc.)	• Carry out 'static electricity and the balloon' experiment • Watch a demonstration of the Van de Graaff generator, including its effect on hair, floating objects and light bulbs

PE:[114]

Topic / sub-topic	Specific knowledge and skills	Specific experiences
Hockey – evasion	• Identifying space through scanning • Creating / exploiting space through good footwork • Running into the space with / without the ball • Supporting the ball carrier • Acceleration / deceleration away from the defender	• A trip to watch a professional hockey match

112 Adapted from: www.berwickshirehighschool.co.uk/attachments/download.asp?file=1065&type=pdf
113 Adapted from: www.coreknowledge.org/wp-content/uploads/2016/09/CKFSequence_Rev.pdf
114 Adapted from: www.berwickshirehighschool.co.uk/attachments/download.asp?file=404&type=pdf

Geography:[115]

Topic / sub-topic	Specific knowledge and skills	Specific experiences
Volcanics	• Key features of a volcano: crater, cone, secondary cone, ash cloud, lava bombs, lava, magma • Mount St Helens (Washington, 1980) and Eyjafjallajökull (Iceland, 2010) • Impact of the eruption - social, economic and environmental	• Watch BBC Volcano Live: Series 1 documentary

Music:[116]

Topic / sub-topic	Specific knowledge and skills	Specific experiences
The orchestra	Families of instruments - strings, brass, woodwinds, percussion: • String family, e.g. violin, viola, cello, double bass • Brass family, e.g. trumpet, French horn, trombone, tuba • Woodwind family, e.g. flute and piccolo (no reeds); clarinet, oboe, bassoon (with reeds) • Percussion family, e.g. drums (timpani, snare), xylophone, wood block, maracas, cymbals, triangle, tambourine	Listen to: • Gioacchino Rossini: 'William Tell Overture', finale (trumpet) • Wolfgang Amadeus Mozart: selections from the 'Horn Concertos' (French horn) • Claude Debussy: 'Prelude to the Afternoon of a Faun' (flute)

115 Adapted from: www.berwickshirehighschool.co.uk/attachments/download.asp?file=1070&type=pdf
116 Adapted from: www.coreknowledge.org/wp-content/uploads/2016/09/CKFSequence_Rev.pdf

Grouping knowledge and skills

In the examples given, 'knowledge' and 'skills' have been grouped together. The reason is that, often, there is an **intrinsic link** between the two and it can be cumbersome (or impossible) for them to be separated. This is especially true for procedural knowledge - knowledge of how to do something.

For example, in the Programme of Teaching and Learning for maths, procedural knowledge and its application are blended in the statement: Multiply whole numbers by 2-digit numbers, e.g. 47 × 12 = 47 × 4 × 3. It doesn't make sense to try to separate these.

Avoid putting limits on how knowledge will be used (where possible)

That said, **where possible**, Programmes of Teaching and Learning should avoid specifying what students should do with their learning. To help understand this point, consider two examples of how a micro curriculum might look in science:

Topic / sub-topic	Specific knowledge and skills	
	Example A	Example B
Chemical reactions	Everyday examples of chemical reactions, including: iron rusting, burning, milk turning sour	State at least two examples of chemical reactions. Identify examples of chemical reactions from a list of different processes (such as glass breaking, paint drying and iron rusting).

Both examples make content clear (which is good). The difference between them relates to the specification of what students are expected **to do** with their learning - Example B gives specification; Example A does not.[117]

117 Example B might be more appropriate as success criteria for a lesson, derived from the content set out in Programmes of Teaching and Learning.

While specification is often a good thing, a risk of specifying the **application of learning** (when we don't need to) is that we put unnecessary limits on this. At its worst, this can lead to teachers 'teaching to the test',[118] by which we mean students are taught **only** things the teacher knows they will be formally assessed on, with teachers making comments such as: 'The reason you need to know this is that it's in the test'.[119] While teachers do need to know how learning will be assessed at the end of units and courses, the details can be made clear in the meso curriculum (as previously discussed) or in separate assessment documentation. Curriculum and assessment aren't the same thing. As much as possible, we shouldn't try to blend them.

Exemplify as much as possible

A further point to highlight about a high-quality micro curriculum is that, as much as possible, there should be **exemplification** to help develop shared meaning. For example, in a Programme of Teaching and Learning for maths, a statement might read: Divide whole numbers up to 100 by a single digit, e.g. 22 ÷ 2, 42 ÷ 6, 88 ÷ 11. Generally, the more examples, the better because examples offer clarity about what teachers should be teaching – and not.

Examples don't put limits on learning – they just make clear what should be included, as a minimum. For example, in English, a Programme of Teaching and Learning for younger students might specify that everyone gets to experience the following stories: *Jack and the Beanstock, Hansel and Gretel* and *The Pied Piper of Hamelin*. Teachers have scope to go beyond these, but the core content for everyone is clear.

118 Kirschner, P.A., Hendrick, C. and Heal, J. (2022) *How Teaching Happens*
119 We want students to want to learn things because they are worth learning, not because they are going to be tested on them.

Linking to pedagogy

While the core purpose of a Programme of Teaching and Learning is to make the **specific content** of the curriculum clear, by including a supplementary 'useful teaching resources' section, these programmes can also support teachers with pedagogy. For example:

Topic / sub-topic	Specific knowledge and skills	Specific experiences	Useful teaching resources
Volcanics	• Key features of a volcano: crater, cone, secondary cone, ash cloud, lava bombs, lava, magma • Mount St Helen's (Washington, 1980) and Eyjafjallajökull (Iceland, 2010) • Impact of the eruption – social, economic and environmental	Watch BBC Volcano Live: Series 1 documentary	• *[This]* PowerPoint presentation • *[This]* section of *[this]* textbook • *[This]* website

Experiences vs pedagogy

As we have previously noted, the dividing line between 'experiences' and 'pedagogy' isn't always clear, but they should nonetheless be thought of separately as much as possible. In Programmes of Teaching and Learning, 'specific experiences' are a core part of the curriculum for everyone and must be included by all teachers. 'Useful teaching resources' are optional, so teachers can decide whether or not these are used.

Focused reflection

- What are your key takeaways from this section?
- If you are a teacher or leader, are there any implications for your teaching or leadership?
- If you are a parent, what questions might you have for your child's school in relation to the points being made?

Curriculum Concept 6: Power up your curriculum using 5Cs

Common pitfall: We don't have a clear strategy to review and develop our curriculum.

The 5Cs of a content-rich curriculum

A 'content-rich' curriculum

Throughout this book, we have been discussing the type of curriculum we should be trying to develop as **knowledge-based**, **skills-orientated** and **experiences-infused**. The catch-all term for curricula of this kind is **content-rich**.[120]

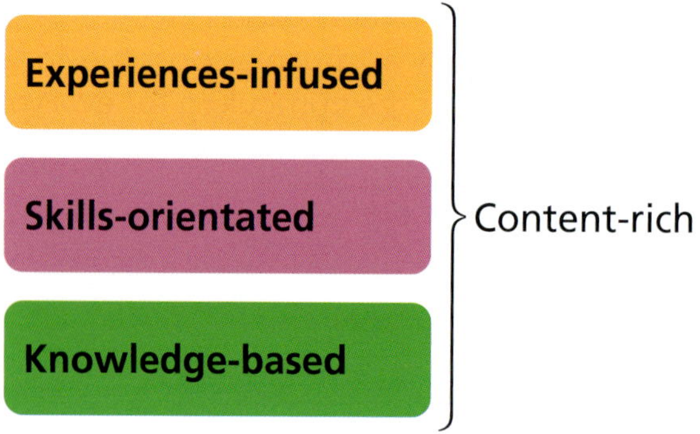

120 Some educationalists talk about a 'knowledge-rich' curriculum, which is effectively the same as a 'knowledge-based' curriculum. I like the phrase 'content-rich' because it captures knowledge, skills and experiences – everything in the 'what' of teaching.

In this final section, we will draw on themes we have explored to this point to unpack how a content-rich curriculum can be developed in your team or school, guided by 5Cs:

1. Clarity
2. Connection
3. Common Challenge
4. Collaboration
5. Change

The 5Cs of a content-rich curriculum:

1. Clarity

The first C of a content-rich curriculum is **clarity**.

A curriculum can be deemed to have clarity if anyone looking at the documentation - including teachers, leaders and parents - can understand what students should be learning and experiencing, **specifically**. No one is left in the dark.

Because national curricula generally don't meet this criterion, it is important that schools **ring-fence time** to develop and update their own Programmes of Teaching and Learning, informed by national guidance. This can be thought of as **curriculum unpacking**.[121]

121 As we discussed in an earlier section, the less specific a national curriculum, the more unpacking a school will have to do.

For example:

National curriculum: An overarching steer

I can compare and contrast a society in the past with my own and contribute to a discussion of the similarities and differences.[122]

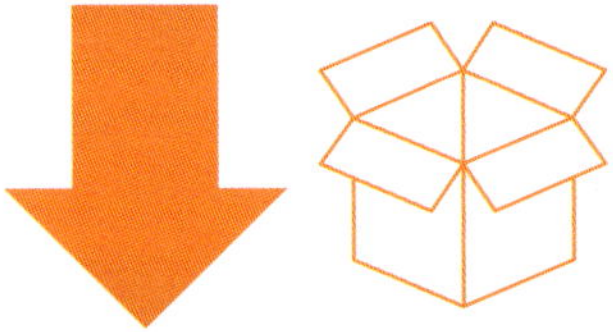

School curriculum: Specific knowledge, skills and experiences

The Aztecs:

- A warrior culture; at its height in the 1400s and early 1500s; the Aztec empire covered much of what is now central Mexico.
- The island city of Tenochtitlan: aqueducts, massive temples.
- Moctezuma (also spelled Montezuma).
- Ruler-priests; practice of human sacrifice.

The impact of an unclear curriculum

On teachers

The less clear the curriculum for a team or school, the less clear teachers are likely to be about what they should be teaching, and so the less focused activities in lessons are likely to be. Teachers can get to the end of a week and think, 'What am I supposed to be teaching next week?'. With little or no clarity,

122 https://education.gov.scot/media/rh3fq1gi/social-studies-eo.pdf

understandably, they will often turn to the internet to find an activity and think, 'That'll do'. Hence, lessons become filled with 'being busy' activities (that keep students occupied – as discussed in Part 1) rather than 'learning' activities (that get students to think about specific things – which is the key to learning). As we have previously said: **curriculum clarity underpins purposeful pedagogy**.

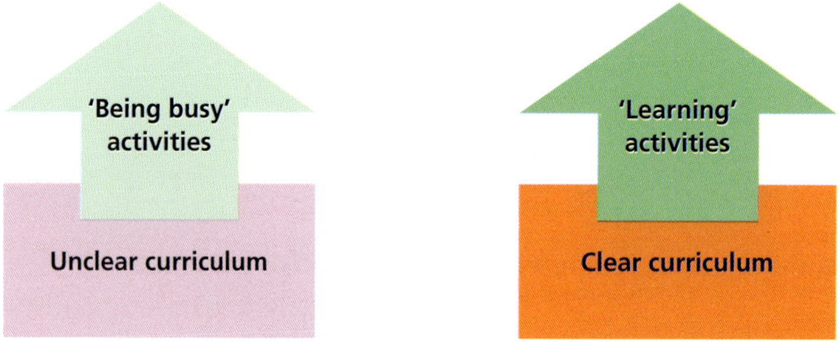

On school leaders

The less clear school leaders are about the content of a school's curriculum, the less certain they can be about what students are learning and how they are progressing. Christine Councell captures this well:

> When the substance of education itself – its object, the thing being learned – is even partly concealed from senior leaders, those leaders must ascertain its quality through proxies, such as the proxy of assessment and results or the proxy of general teaching quality. But therein lie the dangers. Proxies designed to give information about pupils' progress may mislead. Senior and middle leaders commonly discuss which pupils are learning, but such monitoring can be meaningless without attention to **what** pupils are learning.[123]

123 Counsell, C. (2020) 'Better Conversations With Subject Leaders' in Sealy, C. (ed.) *The researchED Guide to The Curriculum*

Mary Myatt builds on this:

> There is no need to have complex tracking systems. Teachers should teach the subject, check through quizzes and reteach if necessary and pupils should be producing a final product which will show what they know, understand and can do, as a result of being taught... Stuart Lock, principal of Bedford Free School, once tweeted: 'If in some schools every meeting on data was replaced with a meeting on the curriculum, those schools would have much better data'.[124]

Great points, and well worth every middle and senior leader reflecting on. Every meeting about data squeezes out the more valuable opportunity to focus on curriculum (and pedagogy).

On students

Ultimately, the group most negatively impacted by an unclear curriculum is students. The less clear the curriculum, the more likely students are to leave school never having had the opportunity to learn or experience things we might reasonably have assumed they would - because there are **hidden gaps** - and the more fragmented their learning is likely to be.

These are the themes we will turn our attention to next.

Focused reflection

- What are your key takeaways from this section?
- If you are a teacher or leader, are there any implications for your teaching or leadership?
- If you are a parent, what questions might you have for your child's school in relation to the points being made?

---

124 Myatt, M. (2020) *The Curriculum*

The 5Cs of a content-rich curriculum:

2. Connection

One of the reasons we need our curriculum to be clear relates to the second C of a content-rich curriculum: **connection**.

When we make connections in the curriculum, we **link topics** we are teaching now to topics that have been taught previously, and topics that are going to be taught in future.

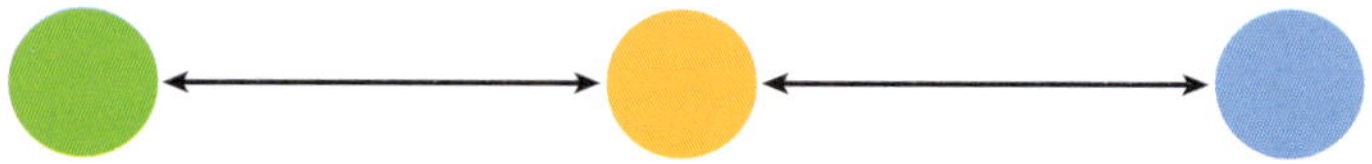

By doing so, we can **strengthen knowledge** and **deepen understanding**.[125] Knowledge gets strengthened as students revisit and rethink about previously taught content, utilising a cognitive principle known as the 'Testing Effect': retrieval strengths memory.[126] Understanding deepens as students build new knowledge into existing schema.

Beyond these reasons, connections can prove **formatively useful** to teachers, with backward links helping us find out where we are starting from. As David Ausubel has said:

> The most important single factor influencing learning is what the learner already knows. Ascertain this and teach [them] accordingly.[127]

125 https://link.springer.com/book/10.1007/978-3-031-74661-1 (Accessed: 26 March 2026)
126 Kirschner, P.A. and Hendrick, C. (2020) *How Learning Happens*
127 Ausubel, D., Novak, J. and Hanesian, H. (1978) *Educational Psychology*

Here again, we see an overlap between curriculum and pedagogy.

Connections create curriculum coherence and avoid fragmentation

By making connections, we can create **curriculum coherence** and **avoid fragmentation**, whereby knowledge is taught in isolation, with no links to anything that has been taught previously or that will be taught in future.[128]

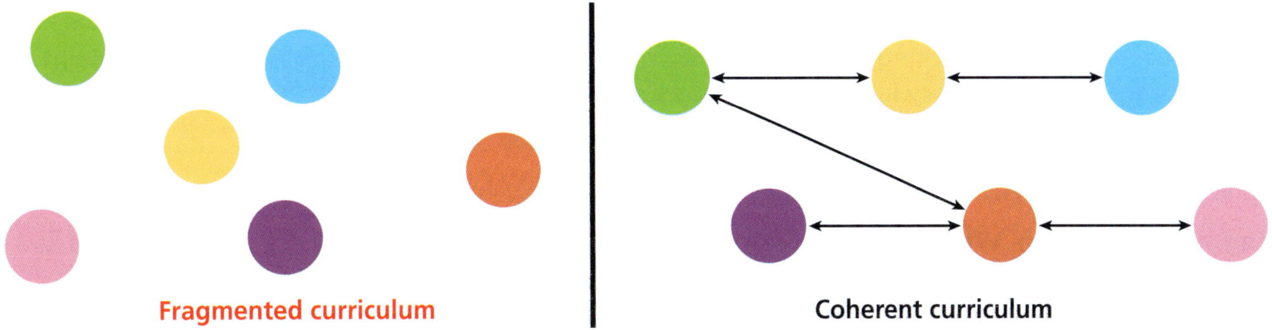

A content-rich curriculum (knowledge-based, skills-orientated and experiences-infused) **isn't a curriculum of isolated facts** – it is a curriculum focused on the development of **deep understanding** and **higher-order thinking**. Connections are the key to the development of both. They can also help close attainment gaps, as highlighted by E.D. Hirsch:

> Knowledge is the key to gap closing, and is best gained coherently by the cumulative, year-by-year study of domains – by a well-defined, cumulative curriculum.[129]

128 https://link.springer.com/book/10.1007/978-3-031-74661-1 (Accessed: 26 March 2026)
129 Hirsch, E.D. (2016) *Why Knowledge Matters*

Careful sequencing

The key to being able to develop connections within and across subjects is to **make content clear** and **sequence it carefully**.[130] Decisions about what to teach at a particular time are made with **past** and **future** content in mind. The thinking of teachers and leaders goes along these lines:

- Because we know students will be taught **[this]** next term, it is sensible to teach **[this]** now.
- Because we know students will be learning about **[this]** next year, it is a good idea to teach them **[this]** now.

For example, a history team noting students will be reading *Animal Farm* in English literature might decide to teach relevant Russian history in advance, to maximise student understanding of the themes being explored.

Why would we teach this now?

Sticking with this theme, **Why would we teach this now?** is a useful question for anyone involved in curriculum sequencing to keep coming back to. As well as helping develop meaningful connections within and between subjects, it can help us avoid the pitfall of teaching potentially useful content at the **wrong time** in a student's schooling.

For example, most people are likely to agree that students should be taught how to create a high-quality CV. However, teaching them to do this when they are in the early years of secondary school is probably

130 Ashbee, R. (2025) 'Defining a knowledge-rich curriculum' in *The value of a knowledge-rich curriculum: An essay collection* [online] Available at: www.civitas.org.uk/publications/knowledge-rich-curriculum (Accessed: 26 March 2026)

the wrong time, because they are unlikely to need to create a CV until the latter years of secondary school.[131] A carefully sequenced curriculum would take account of such considerations.

Within subjects and between subjects

Content connections can be made **within subjects** and **between subjects**.

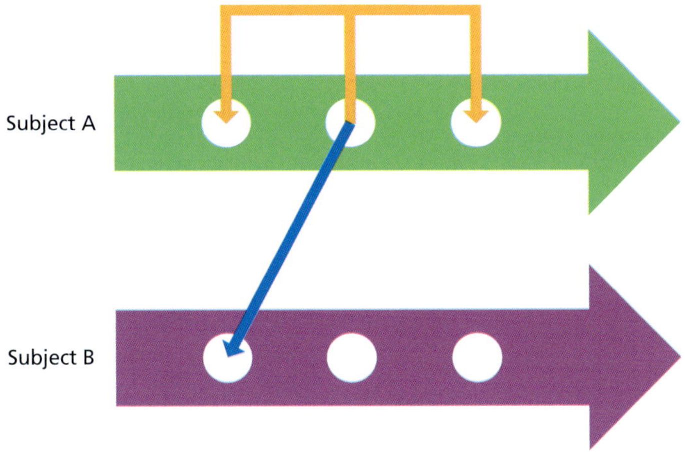

131 This anecdote is based on the real example of a lesson observed where a class of 13-year-old students were being taught to create CVs, almost all of whom would likely have forgotten everything they were taught at the point they were required to apply this knowledge to create a real CV.

Within-subject connections

To appreciate how connections might be made within a subject, consider the following extract from a science curriculum:[132]

	Phase 1	Phase 2	Phase 3
Topic	The human body	The human body	The human body
Sub-topic	Introduction to systems	The digestive system	The skeletal system

Content	• Skeletal system: skeleton, bones, skull
	• Digestive system: mouth, stomach
	• Circulatory system: heart, blood
		• Salivary glands, taste buds
		• Teeth: incisors, canines, bicuspids, molars
		• Oesophagus, stomach, liver, small intestine, large intestine
			• Skeleton, bones, marrow
			• Musculo-skeletal connections
			  ◦ Ligaments
			  ◦ Tendons, Achilles tendon
			  ◦ Cartilage
			• Skull, cranium
			• Spinal column, vertebrae
			• Joints
			• Ribs, rib cage, sternum
			• Scapula (shoulder blades), pelvis, tibia, fibula
			• Broken bones, X-rays

The clarity of content in each phase gives teachers a clear **curriculum route map** helping them understand what (should) have been learned previously and what students will be aiming to learn in future. As well as helping to avoid gaps, this can help avoid unplanned repetition, for example when students are taught the same things about rainforests three years in a row because teachers didn't know what other teachers were teaching. While planned repetition is generally good for learning, unplanned repetition usually just wastes valuable learning time.

132 A 'phase' might mean a topic, term or year stage.

Emma Lennard shares another good example:

> In science, children might grow cress seeds 3 years in a row when they study plants [an example of unplanned and unhelpful repetition]. However, with some thought to the sequencing of content, when learning about plants, children could grow cress seeds, then the following year they could watch mung beans germinate, then the following year they could grow sunflowers. This sequencing, putting curriculum content into a logical order, supports children to learn more, widening and deepening their understanding – for example of plants – over time.[133]

Between-subject connections

To appreciate how connections might be made between subjects, consider the following example:

Geography	English literature	Art
The Mediterranean Region	**Myths and Legends of Ancient Greece and Rome**	**Art of Ancient Rome and Byzantine Civilisation**
• Mediterranean Sea, Aegean Sea, Adriatic Sea • Greece, Italy (peninsula), France, Spain • Strait of Gibraltar, Atlantic Ocean • North Africa, Asia Minor (peninsula), Turkey • Bosporus (strait), Black Sea, Istanbul (Constantinople) • Red Sea, Persian Gulf, Indian Ocean	• Jason and the Golden Fleece • Perseus and Medusa • Cupid and Psyche • The Sword of Damocles • Damon and Pythias • Androcles and the Lion • Horatius at the Bridge	• Artworks of ancient Roman and Byzantine civilisation, including Le Pont du Gard • The Pantheon • Byzantine mosaics • Hagia Sophia

133 Lennard, E. (2025) 'Building A Strong Knowledge-Rich Curriculum' in *The value of a knowledge-rich curriculum: An essay collection* [online] Available at: www.civitas.org.uk/publications/knowledge-rich-curriculum (Accessed: 26 March 2026)

While content could be taught in isolation in each subject, connections between content in different subjects can help enrich learning and make this more memorable. Students can be helped to appreciate how content in one subject relates to that in another, deepening understanding.

Accepting this, a key role for teachers is to help make cross-subject connections explicit, because students are unlikely to make these themselves.[134] To be able to do that, there needs to be clarity about what is being taught in each subject, and when. Hence, the importance of a **clear meso curriculum**, as previously discussed.

Unifying concepts

The identification of **unifying concepts** can be a good way for teachers and leaders to develop connections in the curriculum.[135] For example, 'systems in the human body' might be a useful unifying concept in science. In history, 'democracy' might serve as a useful unifying concept between the Ancient Greeks, Romans and Aztecs.

134 https://link.springer.com/book/10.1007/978-3-031-74661-1 (Accessed: 26 March 2026)
135 Robinson, M. (2022) *Curriculum Revolutions*

The tokenistic theme-day pitfall

All of this said, as with almost everything in education, sound principles can easily morph into unhelpful variants ('lethal mutations'[136]). In this case, an unhelpful variant can be one-off 'thematic days' (sometimes framed as 'interdisciplinary learning'). As a tongue-in-cheek example of how this can easily go wrong, imagine a thematic day on 'water' that looks as follows:[137]

Science	Maths	Art	Technologies	English literature
Students learn about the water cycle.	Students solve problems involving water.	Students draw creatures that live in water.	Students design things that float on water.	Students read *Watership Down.*

While such days are planned with connections in mind (which is good), if the connections are tokenistic and contrived, they are unlikely to enhance learning in any tangible sense. The more likely outcome is that they will waste precious learning time.

136 'Lethal mutations' is a phrase coined by Ed Haertel, referenced in: www.dylanwiliamcenter.com/wp-content/uploads/sites/3/2020/10/DW02-01-Chapter-X-TLC-Paper-03-05-17-Digital.pdf

137 Although tongue-in-cheek, this isn't too far removed from what happens in many schools.

Focused reflection

- What are your key takeaways from this section?
- If you are a teacher or leader, are there any implications for your teaching or leadership?
- If you are a parent, what questions might you have for your child's school in relation to the points being made?

The 5Cs of a content-rich curriculum:

3. Common Challenge

The third C of a content-rich curriculum is actually a double C and stands for **common challenge**.

Challenge

By 'challenge', we mean cognitive engagement (thinking) that includes **appropriate struggle** – not too easy, but not too difficult either. A 'Goldilocks Principle' applies.[138]

To help appreciate this, it can be useful to think of three zones of learning:[139]

Comfort Zone	Healthy-Struggle Zone (AKA: The Goldilocks Zone)	Panic Zone
• Familiar content only • 100% success rates • Challenge too low	• Lots of familiar content, with the staged introduction of content that is unfamiliar • A balance of success and failure, screwed heavily towards success (an 80% success rate is optimal)[140] • The challenge sweet spot	• Lots of unfamiliar content • Low success rates (less than 50%)[141] • Challenge too high

As much as possible, the 'Healthy-Struggle Zone' is the area in which we want students to be.

---

138 Robertson, B. (2021) *The Teaching Delusion 2*
139 Adapted from Allison, S. and Tharby, T. (2015) *Making Every Lesson Count*
140 Rosenshine, B. (2012) 'Principles of Instruction: Research-Based Strategies That All Teachers Should Know'
141 Anything less than 50% is likely to cause students to give up, as discussed in Hattie, J. (2012) *Visible Learning for Teachers*

Common

By 'common', we mean **every student** getting the same opportunity to learn and experience **the same challenging curriculum** for as long as possible at school (as opposed to a curated selection of 'more able' students getting one version of the curriculum, and 'less able' students getting a different version). This principle has three important implications.

Implication 1

By and large, different teachers teaching different classes within the same year group (in the same school) should be teaching the **same content** - though, as we shall go on to discuss, factors such as the levels of support and pace may vary. This means that, typically, different teachers shouldn't be choosing what content to teach a class according to their own interests and preferences.[142] If we allow that to happen - perhaps out of a sense of professional respect to teachers, which is understandable - we increase the likelihood of a 'challenge for some but not for all' scenario.

In *How To Educate A Citizen*, E.D. Hirsch Jr discusses this point:

> The argument for topic commonality as the basis for excellence in early schooling has everything going for it technically: science, data, proof on concept. It lacks only adherence of those who administer our schools, and who have been trained under the late twentieth-century tradition of romantic idealism.[143]

For example, in English literature, if one class is reading *Oliver Twist* while another class in the same year group is reading *Holes*, almost certainly one class is experiencing a more challenging curriculum than the other. As a result, we get avoidable learning and achievement gaps.

142 Although, as we have previously noted, it is usually sensible for there to be some scope for teachers to go beyond the core school curriculum.

143 Hirsch, E.D., Jr (2020) *How To Educate A Citizen*

Implication 2

The second implication is that **we shouldn't let students specialise in learning too early in their schooling**. While there **will** come a point when the curriculum should be differentiated – for example, because students are ready to specialise in particular academic or vocational subjects – that point should be relatively late in schooling.[144] If it comes too early, students will miss out on learning and experiences they would likely find valuable, and that they aren't guaranteed to get from home. In *Cleverlands*, Lucy Crehan argues that the age for curriculum specialisation should be 15,[145] which I think is about right. To that point, all students should be learning a broad, common curriculum.[146]

Implication 3

The third implication is that we need to **avoid in-class ability grouping and between-class setting** as much as possible, for as long as possible. Once we start to segregate students – such as by putting them into 'most able' or 'least able' ability groups or classes – we start to create learning and achievement gaps between the different groups and classes. This is the antithesis of what schools should be trying to do. Through high-quality teaching, we should be trying to close learning and achievement gaps between students from advantaged and less-advantaged homes.

The *What Makes Great Teaching?* evidence review discusses this, making clear that ability groupings and setting can typically exacerbate learning gaps by holding learning back unnecessarily; create low-aspiration mindsets; and develop stigmas directed at those grouped as 'lower ability':

> Evidence on the effects of grouping by ability, either by allocating students to different classes, or to within-class groups, suggests that it makes very little difference to learning outcomes. Although

---

144 Note: vocational curriculum pathways are as important as academic pathways.
145 Crehan, L. (2016) *Cleverlands*
146 Unless there are significant barriers or very good reasons for them not to be.

ability grouping can in theory allow teachers to target a narrower range of pace and content of lessons, it can also create an exaggerated sense of within-group homogeneity and between-group heterogeneity in the teacher's mind. This can result in teachers failing to make necessary accommodations for the range of different needs within a supposedly homogeneous 'ability' group, and over-doing their accommodations for different groups, going too fast with the high-ability groups and too slow with the low.[147]

With all of this in mind, I would suggest the take-away should be: **Don't group students by ability (in or between classes) unless you really have to.**[148]

The point, 'unless you really have to', is important to add as a caveat. The reason is that, sometimes, the gap between different students becomes so big that teachers can't reasonably be expected to accommodate it. However, it needs to be stressed that this situation should be viewed as the **exception**, not the rule. In most subjects throughout the primary and early secondary-school stages of schooling, students can and should be taught in 'mixed-ability classes' (they don't need to be 'set' or 'streamed').

147 www.suttontrust.com/wp-content/uploads/2019/12/What-makes-great-teaching-FINAL-4.11.14-1.pdf

148 The one exception I would be prepared to accept can be maths, owing to the particular way knowledge builds on knowledge in this subject. If there are significant, pre-existing knowledge gaps between different students in maths, some form of setting might be the best approach for everyone. However, two key points to keep in mind are: **1** we should be doing everything we can to avoid these gaps in the proceeding years of schooling and **2** the aim of any 'lower set' class should be to catch up the other classes as much as possible. Accepting this, if your school has setting, the very best teachers should be the ones assigned to the students who need these the most.

Progress towards common, challenging learning goals

Across a year group, we want learning to look more like this...

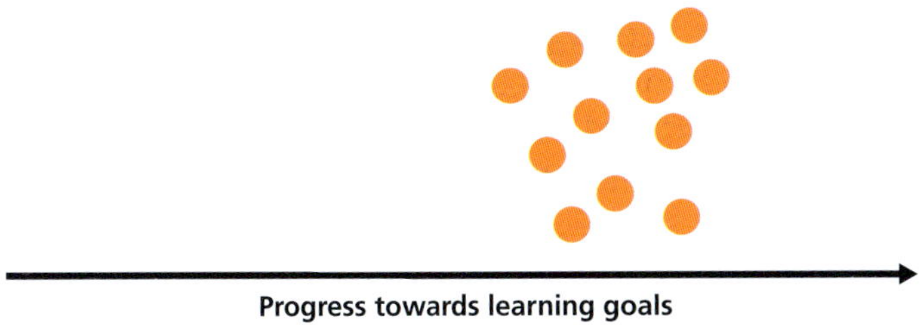

...than like this:

Our aim should be to help **everyone** achieve common, challenging learning goals. Some classes might go a little faster than others and some students will almost certainly need more support than others, but for the most part, the curriculum should be the same.

If we don't do that and instead differentiate what students are taught, many students will access knowledge, skills and experiences that many others never get. Hence, we get the learning, achievement and experience gaps we are trying to avoid and close.

Differentiate the support and challenge

Accepting this, rather than differentiating the curriculum in the early to mid stages of schooling, or using 'all...', 'some...' and 'a few...' learning intentions in lessons, we should focus on **differentiating the support**[149] available to students and the opportunities they have to apply their knowledge and skills through **differentiated challenge**. In other words, there should be:

- **a core curriculum for everyone**, with common learning goals
- **core success criteria** for everyone (the things students must be able to do to prove their learning), with **differentiated support**
- **opportunities for students to go beyond the success criteria** for everyone - **differentiated challenge** - so no one's learning is held back.

149 Hattie, J. (2009) *Visible Learning for Teachers*

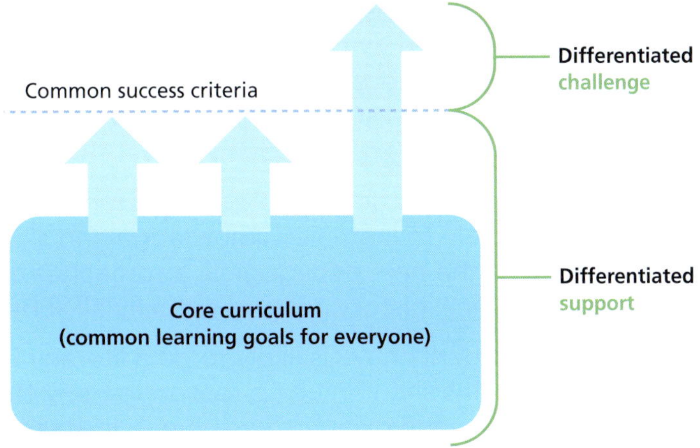

Be aware of categorising students by levels

It is with all of this in mind that teachers and schools should **be wary about categorising students by levels**. For example, in Scotland, the 3–15 phase of the curriculum is organised as five levels: Early, First, Second, Third and Fourth. When students move from primary to secondary school, most are expected to have 'achieved' the Second level and be ready to begin the Third – they are often labelled 'Third level students'. However, in part because approaches to assessing 'achievement of a level' are so unreliable, and in part because no one really seems to understand what 'achieving a level' means anyway (I include myself here), many students aren't tracked as having 'achieved the Second level' by the time they start secondary school. These students are often labelled 'First level students' or 'Second level students', and teachers will sometimes complain about having to teach First, Second and Third level students in the same class.

However, in reality, these levels often mean very little and so don't warrant much attention. In most cases, First, Second and Third level students **are** able to learn new knowledge and skills equally well in the same class, so long as the curriculum is clear and the best pedagogical approaches are used. This applies as much to English literature as it does to science, history, art and virtually all subjects.

The barrier some First and Second level students have is likely to be a literacy barrier – their reading and / or writing abilities are relatively poor – but this shouldn't be a reason to deny them access to knowledge, skills and experiences in science, history, art... and every other subject. In-lesson pedagogies need to take account of any literacy barriers, and there should be out-of-class interventions to help students to read and write.

In place of levels, student progress would be much better assessed via regular in-class informal assessment, with periodic formal approaches, the results of which can be shared directly (for example, as a raw score).[150, 151] For any of this to happen, there needs to be a clear curriculum.

150 See Appendix 2 for a fuller overview of assessment.

151 Such an approach isn't at odds with periodic standardised assessments at a national level to benchmark performance, so long as such assessments aren't used to categorise students or rank schools in league tables.

Focused reflection

- What are your key takeaways from this section?
- If you are a teacher or leader, are there any implications for your teaching or leadership?
- If you are a parent, what questions might you have for your child's school in relation to the points being made?

The 5Cs of a content-rich curriculum:

4. Collaboration

The fourth C of a content-rich curriculum is **collaboration**.

By 'collaboration', we mean that content is **discussed**, **debated** and **agreed**. Nothing is off the table for inclusion in the curriculum, but nothing is guaranteed either. Such conversations can help focus minds on the best order to teach content, which links to the points we made previously about curriculum sequencing.[152]

Who should be involved?

Teachers and leaders should all have voices in the collaborative process, and there can be scope for student and parent voices too. Curriculum design should be seen as a whole-school enterprise.[153]

For example, to support student and parental engagement, there could be periodic surveys that ask questions such as: 'What, if anything, do you think is missing from our curriculum?'. Answers might reveal some novel ideas that school staff might not have considered, and that might add value. Not everyone will contribute, but at least everyone has the opportunity.

Curriculum Development Meetings

To support teacher engagement, leaders need to **ringfence time** for collaborative curriculum development. For example, in place of the traditional team or department meetings (that often focus on administrative matters and student tracking data), there could be weekly, fortnightly or monthly

152 Lennard, E. (2025) 'Building A Strong Knowledge-Rich Curriculum'
153 Almond, N. (2020) 'Curriculum Coherence: How Best to Do It?'

Curriculum Development Meetings that focus on the meso and micro curriculum (as previously discussed). Senior leaders can take part in discussions, or build similar meetings into their own calendars.

In general, it is sensible for these meetings to take the following form:

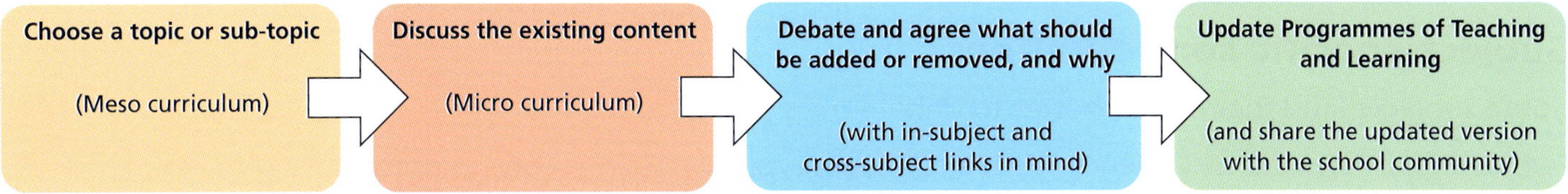

You can't leave your subject or school without...

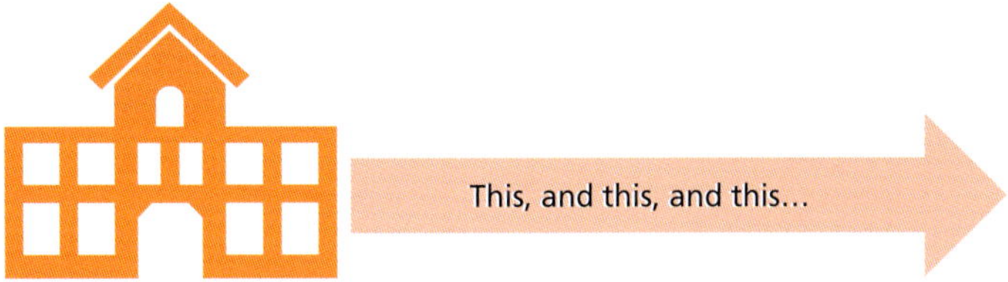

As a stimulus for discussions and debates, it can be helpful for teachers and leaders to consider the **core knowledge**, **skills** and **experiences** no student should be able to leave a subject or the school without.[154] For example, members of a team might discuss:

154 Robertson, B. (2021) *The Teaching Delusion 2*

- After X number of years learning in our subject or school, what should **all students** know, be able to do or have experienced?[155]
- After X number of years learning in our subject or school, what **can't you leave without** having learned or experienced?

Subject-specific considerations

Some subjects lend themselves better to debate than others.

For example, in maths and science, where concepts typically build on one another through 'vertical connections', certain topics need to be taught before another. The debate isn't so much **whether** something should be taught, but **when**. In other subjects, such as history and English literature, where concepts might link to one another through 'horizontal connections' but don't necessarily build, there is more scope for debate about **what** the specific content is.[156]

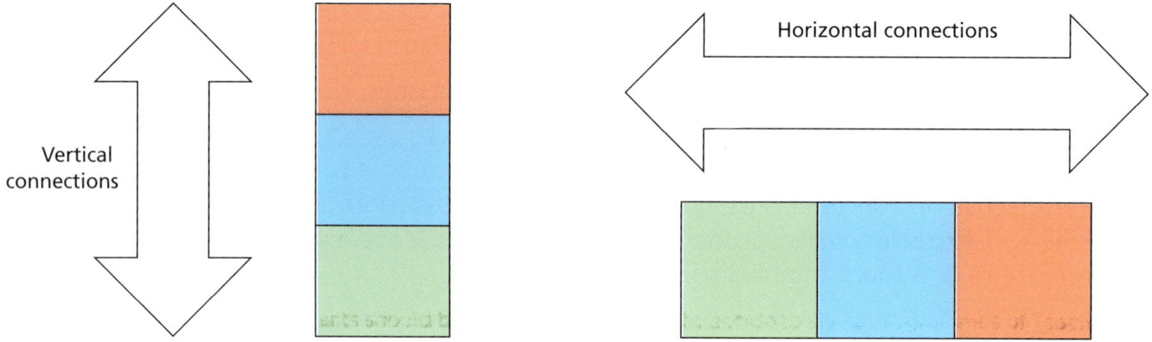

155 Adapted from Percival, A. (2020) 'Curriculum Building in a Primary School'
156 Ashbee, R. (2020) 'Why It's So Important to Understand School Subjects – And How We Might Begin to Do So'

Examples

If we take geography as an example, the conversation might go along the following lines:

Question	Possible answer
Do we want students to know the **names of every continent**?	Yes
Okay, so do we want students to know **where the continents are** in relation to each other?	Yes
Okay, so do we want students to know the **names of every country in every continent**?	No
Okay, so do we want students to know the names of **some countries in some continents**?	Yes
Okay, so **which countries, and why**?	Lots of discussion...

A conversation about the English literature curriculum might take the following form:

Question	Possible answer
Should all students learn about a **Shakespeare play**?	Yes
Okay, so does everyone need to learn about the **same play**?	No
Okay, so are we going to agree a **pool** teachers can choose from?	Yes
Okay, so **which plays, and why**?	Lots of discussion...

Content Cues

Content Cues offer a helpful stimulus for discussions in Curriculum Development Meetings. These are statements designed to get teachers and leaders talking about specific themes. For example:[157]

1. The building blocks that students will need if they decide to specialise in this subject in future
2. The 'big' concepts and ideas, the character of which varies among subjects
3. The major works of major people, which, too, can mean different things in different subjects (such as writers, performers, inventors, and so on)
4. The knowledge students are likely to need to understand, appreciate and look after the world around them, and beyond
5. The knowledge students are likely to need to understand, appreciate and look after themselves, and others
6. Key dates and timelines
7. Key vocabulary, including the etymology of words
8. Knowledge and experiences that subject teachers believe are 'interesting'

Don't fall into the 'useful pitfall'

As content is discussed, debated and agreed, teachers and leaders should be careful not to fall into the **useful pitfall**, whereby we consider only content we believe students are likely to find useful, such as in the world of work (this is something we highlighted in an earlier section, but it is a point worth re-emphasising).

157 Robertson, B. (2021) *The Teaching Delusion 2*

Skills for work

One reason is that much of the 'in-the-job' knowledge and skills that students might require for a particular line of work can (and should) be taught once they are in that job. Too often in my experience, skills for work are overemphasised in schools.[158] For the most part, schools should focus on teaching students things **they are unlikely to learn elsewhere** or **might never get the opportunity or have the inclination** to learn again.

Hibernating knowledge and skills

Another reason is that we often have no idea what knowledge and skills students will find useful in life. Much of what we teach them will be **hibernating** for periods of time (sometimes years), only to become useful at future, unexpected points in life. For example, as an adult, a former student might be reading an article, watching a documentary or visiting an exhibition, and suddenly things they had been taught at school become useful in helping them understand and appreciate what they are seeing and hearing now.

Taking my own schooling as an example, when my English teacher, Mrs Norris, announced that we were going to spend the next six weeks learning about the poems of Philip Larkin, had the classroom not been on the second floor, I would have been straight out the window.[159] 'I don't like poetry and I don't care about Philip Larkin' was my (silent) reactionary mindset. 'I'm never going to use any of this knowledge, so what's

158 This is especially true when primary-school teachers feel pressured to link learning to work.

159 Anecdotally, a student in my year at school did jump out the window of a ground-floor German language classroom, so determined were they to avoid the learning that day. The most worrying aspect of this anecdote was – the teacher never actually noticed they had gone!

the point in learning it?' However, much to my amazement, I actually enjoyed learning about these poems. My teacher made the content interesting, which is a hallmark of all great teachers. What's more, knowledge that I didn't believe at the time would ever be useful became useful later in life in ways that I couldn't have predicted. For example, every so often I come across Philip Larkin's work as I am reading or watching something. Knowing something about this helps me understand and appreciate more of what I am reading and watching. Knowledge that had been hibernating woke up unexpectedly and enhanced the moment.

Cultural capital

The concept of 'hibernating knowledge' links closely with **cultural capital**, by which we mean the extent to which people can make sense of things they are seeing and hearing in films, books, exhibitions, pieces of music, and so on, as a result of the knowledge they have stored in long-term memory.

When they read articles in newspapers and online platforms, we want students to have enough cultural capital to understand what they are reading, to know the differences between facts and opinions, to be able to form opinions of their own, to recognise biases, and so on. When they visit a museum or gallery, we want them to have cultural capital so they can really appreciate what they are seeing and get the most from the experience. While it is true that anyone could visit a museum or gallery and get a lot from it without having much background knowledge, relevant background knowledge will almost certainly make experiences more interesting, memorable and enjoyable, the importance of which shouldn't be underestimated.

Powerful knowledge

It is with all of this in mind that Michael Young and David Lambert, strong proponents of social justice, suggest schools should focus on teaching students **powerful knowledge**, by which they mean knowledge that takes them beyond their lived experiences, opening a wider world.[160] Students from every home should get equal access to the same powerful knowledge through the school curriculum, which is one of the most significant things a school can do to address the very real background disadvantages that many students have, through no fault of their own. As we have said many times throughout this book: schools should be doing as much as can reasonably be expected to close achievement and experience gaps. By doing so, they transform lives.

Students don't know what they don't know

Accepting this, it is often a mistake to let students decide what to learn at school for the simple reason that it is impossible for them to know what they don't know. Given the choice not to learn about Philip Larkin at school, I would know virtually nothing about his work today. The same principle applies to a great deal of what I was taught at school. There were lots of topics I wasn't particularly bothered about learning, but today I am very glad that my teachers pushed, encouraged and supported me to learn everything they did. I have a lot more cultural capital and powerful knowledge than I would have otherwise (and had the curriculum been *even better*, I would almost certainly have *even more*).

In saying this, we aren't suggesting there is **no room** for student voice in the curriculum. As we discussed earlier, there can and should be opportunities for students (and parents) to put forward suggestions as to what to include in our school curriculum, such as through surveys and focus groups. Nor is it to say students shouldn't have a lot of choice in deciding **what they do** with the things they are learning,

160 Young, M. and Lambert, D. (2014) *Knowledge and the Future School*

including through open-ended activities such as debates and extended writing – these are important pedagogical approaches. It is simply to make the point that **teachers are the subject experts** and, for that reason, **teachers** are generally the people best placed to make decisions about the best content to include in the school curriculum (in circumstances where there are decisions to be made, as discussed in Part 1).

Focused reflection

- What are your key takeaways from this section?
- If you are a teacher or leader, are there any implications for your teaching or leadership?
- If you are a parent, what questions might you have for your child's school in relation to the points being made?

The 5Cs of a content-rich curriculum:

5. Change

The fifth and final C of a content-rich curriculum stands for **change**.

By 'change', we mean that the content of the school curriculum **evolves over time**. Where we see gaps, we fill these. Where we see opportunities for meaningful in-subject and cross-subject connections, we make these. If we feel there is too much content, we remove things. And so on. Such decisions will never be easy, but we need to accept that because we can't teach *everything* that might be valuable, choices need to be made about what is ***most* valuable**.[161]

Breadth or depth?

This latter point brings us to the final question we will consider in this book, which is: **Should our curriculum focus more on breadth or depth?**

While this can be argued either way, on balance, the best steer is generally: **start broad and go deeper later**.[162]

161 Myatt, M. (2018) *The Curriculum*
162 Jenkins, S. (2018) *A Short History of Europe*

On that basis, in the early to mid stages of schooling, the mantra 'fewer things in greater depth' is usually a mistaken one.[163] A wider pool of knowledge will almost certainly be more useful to most students in primary and early secondary school, helping them to understand and do more across more subjects.[164] It will also help them become better readers, because people who are the best readers are generally those who know a lot about a lot.[165]

As students move towards the latter stages of secondary education, the steer should flip to become 'depth over breath'. This principle links to research that suggests in countries with the highest-performing educational programmes, the focus is generally on fewer topics in a deeper, more profound manner.[166]

In a nutshell, as we said in Curriculum Concept 5: **start with the big picture and work your way in**. That way, your curriculum is likely to be as powerful as possible.

---

163 Robinson, M. (2022) *Curriculum Revolutions*

164 Although, like anything, we can obviously take this too far. If we overemphasise breadth, we risk superficial learning that becomes little more than a list of facts about lots of topics, which isn't what a content-rich curriculum should look like.

165 Christodoulou, D. (2013) *Seven Myths About Education*

166 https://link.springer.com/book/10.1007/978-3-031-74661-1 (Accessed: 26 March 2026)

Focused reflection

- What are your key takeaways from this section?
- If you are a teacher or leader, are there any implications for your teaching or leadership?
- If you are a parent, what questions might you have for your child's school in relation to the points being made?

Afterword: Put your curriculum on a pedestal

Through high-quality teaching of a high-quality curriculum, schools transform lives. The better our teaching and the better our curriculum, the more powerful this transformation is likely to be.

Accepting this, the **specific content** and **sequencing** of a school's curriculum should be high on the list of 'regular attention priorities' for middle and senior leaders,[167] and teachers need to be given regular blocks of time to focus on the continuous improvement of the curriculum. Other things that we might have once believed to be important - but we now realise aren't **as** important - will likely need to go. Curriculum and pedagogy should be put on a priority pedestal that (almost) nothing else should be allowed to sit on.

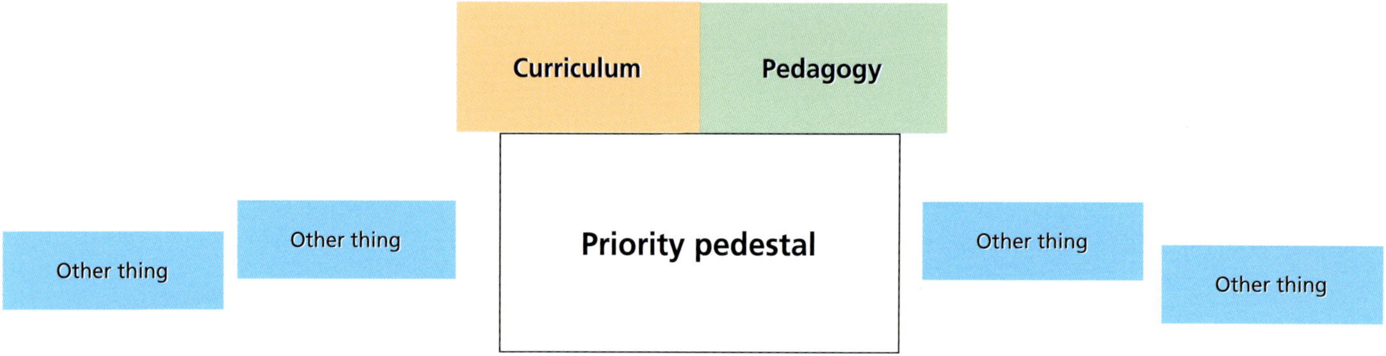

If this book has achieved what it intended, you will feel fired up and empowered to play a key role in helping to make the curriculum in your team or school ***even better*** than it is already.

Power up your curriculum and watch every student's learning power up too.

167 Myatt, M. (2020) *The Curriculum*

Appendix 1: An overview of pedagogical principles

Pedagogically, most things usually work to some extent, but not everything works equally well all the time.[168]

The principles summarised in this appendix are designed to support teachers to make good decisions about the best things to do – or not do – as they plan and deliver lessons, with '**best learning bets**' in mind.[169]

Principle 1	**The most important consideration is the extent to which all students are learning what we plan for them to learn.**	When we plan lessons, the most important consideration should be what, specifically, we want students to learn. If we aren't clear, it's very unlikely our students will be. Clarity in our own minds should lead to clearer learning intentions and success criteria, and to lesson activities focused on achieving both.
Principle 2	**Learning usually requires deliberate effort.**	Learning doesn't tend to happen by diffusion. Just because students see or hear things, they won't necessarily learn them. Paying attention is a prerequisite to learning, but there usually needs to be more. That 'more' is thinking about specific things in a deliberate way. Thinking is the key to learning.
Principle 3	**We need to plan with working memory and long-term memory in mind.**	It is helpful to think of our brains as having two memory compartments: working memory, where thinking happens, and long-term memory, where learning happens. Thinking promotes learning by encouraging transfer between these two compartments.
Principle 4	**Being busy and learning are not the same thing.**	When considering lessons, it can be useful to draw a distinction between 'learning' activities and 'being busy' activities. 'Learning' activities get students to think about specific things. 'Being busy' activities, e.g. copying, don't do this. Aim to keep 'being busy' activities to a minimum and for learning activities to dominate.

168 Hattie, J. (2012) *Visible Learning for Teachers*
169 These are derived from the principles discussed in Robertson, B. (2021) *The Teaching Delusion 2*.

Principle 5	**Desirable difficulties propel learning forward.**	When designing learning activities, keep the 'Goldilocks Principle' in mind: *not too easy* but *not too difficult*. We should be trying to create 'desirable difficulties',[170] moving learning forward via appropriate and increasing levels of challenge.
Principle 6	**A teaching–learning gap is inevitable (but reducible).**	Because learning doesn't tend to happen by diffusion, a teaching learning gap is usually inevitable.[171] The best teacher presentation, explanation or demonstration in the world won't necessarily lead to learning. Content coverage and effective teaching aren't the same thing. Continuous formative assessment is the key to both measuring and to closing the teaching–learning gap.
Principle 7	**The learning of one or two students tells us nothing about the learning of everyone.**	It's easy to fall into the trap of using evidence of learning from one or two students as a proxy for everyone. However, over-generalising risks leaving many behind. Regular use of show-me boards is a great way to address this. Show-me boards help make *all* students' learning visible and are an invaluable formative tool.
Principle 8	**Producing product doesn't necessarily evidence learning.**	Learning is the development of long-term memory. If we want to check what students have learned, tasks should get students to do something using long-term memory. If long-term memory is side-lined, such as when students make posters with notes in front of them, we should question whether it's learning we are seeing.
Principle 9	**The best way to teach novices is different from the best way to teach experts.**	Anyone starting to learn anything new in a particular area is a relative novice. As knowledge develops in long-term memory, people become more expert in this area. Because of the differences in the knowledge they have, novices think differently from experts. This means novices need to be taught differently from experts.[172]
Principle 10	**Effective teaching blends Specific and Non-specific Teaching approaches.**	*Specific Teaching* means direct-interactive instruction infused with continuous formative assessment.[173] This is usually the most effective and efficient way to teach novices. As expertise develops, *Non-specific Teaching* will often become more effective. Now, students are in a better position to lead their learning more.

170 Bjork, E.L. and Bjork, R.A. (2014) 'Making Things Hard on Yourself, But in a Good Way'
171 Wiliam, D. and Leahy, S. (2015) *Embedding Formative Assessment*
172 Kirschner, P.A. and Hendrick, C. (2020) *How Learning Happens*
173 Robertson, B. (2020) *The Teaching Delusion*

Appendix 2: An overview of assessment principles

Assessment is concerned with checking the extent to which something has been understood or learned. This can be done **informally** or **formally**, and the information we glean can be used **formatively** or **summatively**.

Informal and formal

Informal assessment is the most common type in teaching. Examples include in-lesson questioning and observation of practice. Because these sorts of assessments (checks) **don't count for much**, they can be thought of as 'informal' (low stakes).[174]

Formal assessment is more periodic. Examples include end-of-topic tests and exams. Because these sorts of assessments (checks) **do count for something**, such as determining topic or end-of-course grades, they can be thought of as 'formal' (higher stakes).

174 Some people talk about such assessment as 'no stakes'.

Formative and summative

The information that comes from assessments (informal or formal) can be used formatively, summatively or in both ways.[175]

- When used **formatively**, assessment information **guides actions** by teachers (responsive teaching) or students (responsive study) about what to do next.
- When used **summatively**, assessment information is used to **reach judgements** by teachers or students about performance or progress (changes in performance over time).

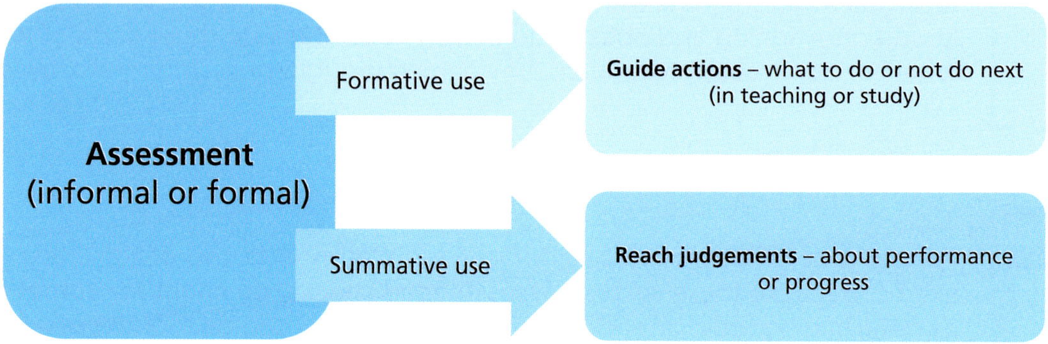

A key point to emphasise here is that the terms *formative* and *summative* are best thought of in relation to **how assessment information is used**, rather than an assessment itself.[176]

175 Although, in practice, the dividing lines between these two are often blurred, as highlighted in Kirschner, P.A., Hendrick, C. and Heal, J. (2022) How Teaching Happens.

176 Wiliam, D. and Leahy, S. (2015) Embedding Formative Assessment

Dual functions

In reality, most assessment information can be used **both** formatively and summatively. However, the extent to which it is **better suited** to one function or another will depend on the nature of the information.[177]

Scores

Taking a score from an end-of-topic assessment as an example (such as 20 out of 30), a **summative function** of this information would be if it is used by the teacher or by a student to reach a judgement about performance or progress.[178] A **formative function** would be if it encourages the student to re-study the parts of the topic they got wrong, or leads to the teacher reteaching the aspects of this topic that weren't done well.[179]

Comments

The same principles apply to written and verbal comments. For example, 'You need to improve your use of full stops' is a comment that has more of a **summative function** than formative (it is *summing up*). If the comment included details about how to improve your use of full stops, the **formative function** would be increased.

177 Christodoulou, D. (2016) *Making Good Progress?*

178 If this is completed in practice conditions, this is informal assessment. If it is completed in real test conditions, this is formal assessment. The point being: end-of-topic tests can be used informally and formally, with the information emerging from them used summatively and formatively.

179 www.tes.com/magazine/analysis/secondary/making-sense-formative-assessment-school-leader-sqa-exams (Accessed: 26 March 2026)

The link to specificity

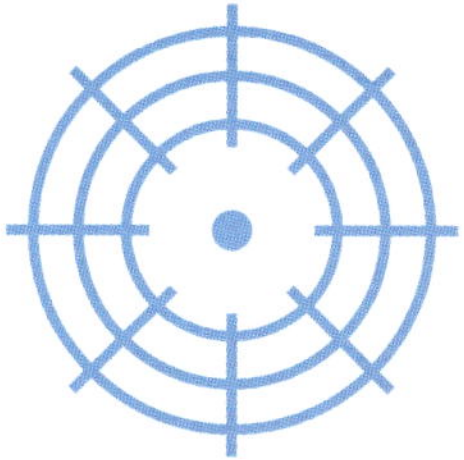

In general, the **more specific the content** that assessment information relates to, the more useful this should be **formatively** (and the less so summatively). The **broader the body of content** that assessment information relates to, the more useful this should be **summatively** (and the less so formatively).

To appreciate this, imagine an end-of-topic assessment that has been carefully designed so that each task targets specific knowledge or skills. The teacher records students' performance in **each task** and in the assessment **as a whole**, as follows:

	Task 1 (/2)	**Task 2 (/3)**	**Task 3 (/3)**	**Total /8**
Student A	2	0	3	**5**
Student B	2	0	3	**5**
Student C	1	1	3	**5**
Class average	**1.6**	**0.3**	**3**	**5**

↑ Tasks 1–3: **Formative use**

↑ Total: **Summative use**

As we have discussed, all this information can be used **both** summatively and formatively. However, it isn't all **equally valuable** for both purposes. The **task-by-task scores** (which target specific knowledge and skills) should be more useful **formatively** than summatively; the **total scores** (which cover a much broader range of knowledge and skills) should be more useful **summatively** than formatively.

References

Allison, S. and Tharby, A. (2015) *Making Every Lesson Count*. Crown House Publishing: Carmarthen.

Almond, N. (2020) 'Curriculum Coherence: How Best to Do It?' in Sealy, C. (ed.) *The researchED Guide to The Curriculum*. Woodbridge: John Catt Educational Ltd, pp.59–70.

Ashbee, R. (2020) 'Why It's So Important to Understand School Subjects – And How We Might Begin to Do So' in Sealy, C. (ed.) *The researchED Guide to The Curriculum*. Woodbridge: John Catt Educational Ltd, pp.31–40.

Ashman, G. (2022) *Cognitive Load Theory*. London: Corwin UK.

Ausubel, D., Novak, J. and Hanesian, H. (1978) *Educational Psychology: A Cognitive View* (2nd edn). New York, NY: Holt McDougal.

Badger, C. and Firth, J. (2025) *Creativity for Teachers*. Abingdon: Routledge.

Bjork, E.L. and Bjork, R.A. (2014) 'Making Things Hard on Yourself, But in a Good Way: Creating Desirable Difficulties to Enhance Learning' in Gernsbacher, M.A. and Pomerantz, J. (eds) *Psychology and The Real World: Essays Illustrating Fundamental Contributions to Society* (2nd edn). New York, NY: Worth, pp.59–68.

Brown, P.C., Roediger III, H.L. and McDaniel, M.A. (2014) *Make It Stick: The Science of Successful Learning*. Holland, Ohio: Dreamscape Media, LLC.

Bryson, B. (2025) *A Short History of Nearly Everything 2.0*. London: Penguin.

Christodoulou, D. (2014) *Seven Myths About Education*. Oxon: Routledge.

Christodoulou, D. (2017) *Making Good Progress?: The future of Assessment for Learning*. Oxford: Oxford University Press.

Conklin, P.L., Pallanca, R.L. and Smirnoff, N. (1997) 'L-ascorbic acid metabolism in the ascorbate-deficient arabidopsis mutant vtc1, Plant Physiol 115(3)', pp.1277–1285 in National Library of Medicine [online] Available at: www.ncbi.nlm.nih.gov/pubmed/9390448 (Accessed 18 December 2025).

Counsell, C. (2020) 'Better Conversations With Subject Leaders' in Sealy, C. (ed.) *The researchED Guide to The Curriculum*. Woodbridge: John Catt Educational Ltd, pp.95–121.

Crehan, L. (2016) *Cleverlands: The Secrets Behind the Success of the World's Education Superpowers*. London: Unbound.

Hattie, J. (2012) *Visible Learning for Teachers: Maximizing Impact on Learning*. Vermont: Echo Point Books & Media, LLC.

Heal, J. and Berlin, R. (2025) *Mental Models: How understanding the mind can transform the way you work and learn*. London: Hachette Learning.

Hendrick, C. and Macpherson, R. (2017) *What Does This Look Like in the Classroom? Bridging the Gap Between Research and Practice*. Woodbridge: John Catt Educational Ltd.

Hirsch, E.D. (2016) *Why Knowledge Matters: Rescuing Our Children from Failed Educational Theories*. Cambridge, MA: Harvard Education Press.

Hirsch, E.D., Jr (2020) *How to Educate a Citizen*. New York, NY: HarperCollins.

Howard, K. and Hill, C. (2020) *Symbiosis: The Curriculum and the Classroom*. Woodbridge: John Catt Educational Ltd.

Jenkins, S. (2019) *A Short History of Europe: From Pericles to Putin*. London: Penguin.

Kirschner, P.A. and Hendrick, C. (2024) *How Learning Happens: Seminal Works in Educational Psychology and What They Mean in Practice.* Oxon: Routledge.

Kirschner, P.A., Hendrick, C. et al (2022) How Teaching Happens: Seminal Works in Teaching and Teacher *Effectiveness and What They Mean in Practice.* Oxon: Routledge.

Kirschner, P.A., Sweller, J. and Clark, R.E. (2010) 'Why minimal guidance during instruction does not work: An analysis of the failure of constructivist, discovery, problem-based, experiential, and inquiry-based teaching' in *Educational Psychologist*, 41(2): pp.75–86.

Kirschner, P.A., Hendrick, C. and Heal, J. (2025) *Instructional Illusions.* London: Hachette Learning.

Lemov, D. (2021) *Teach Like a Champion 3.0: 63 Techniques that Put Students on the Path to College.* San Francisco, CA: Jossey-Bass.

Lennard, E. (2025) 'Building A Strong Knowledge-Rich Curriculum' in *The value of a knowledge-rich curriculum: An essay collection* [online] Available at: www.civitas.org.uk/publications/knowledge-rich-curriculum (Accessed: 26 March 2026).

Myatt, M. (2018) *The Curriculum: Gallimaufry to coherence.* Woodbridge: John Catt Educational Ltd.

Paterson, L. (2026) *Lessons from Scottish Schools: Why Knowledge Matters.* Edinburgh: Edinburgh University Press.

Percival, A. (2020) 'Curriculum Building in a Primary School' in Sealy, C. (ed.) *The researchED Guide to The Curriculum.* Woodbridge: John Catt Educational Ltd, pp.71–84.

Reid, A. (2020) 'Cultural Capital, Critical Theory and Curriculum' in Sealy, C. (ed.) *The researchED Guide to The Curriculum.* Woodbridge: John Catt Educational Ltd, pp.41–48.

Robertson, B. (2020) *The Teaching Delusion: Why teaching in our schools isn't good enough (and how we can make it better).* Woodbridge: John Catt Educational Ltd.

Robertson, B. (2021) *The Teaching Delusion 2: Teaching Strikes Back.* Woodbridge: John Catt Educational Ltd.

Robertson, B. (2023) *Power Up Your Pedagogy: The Illustrated Handbook of Teaching.* Woodbridge: John Catt Educational Ltd.

Robinson, M. (2022) *Curriculum Revolutions: A practical guide to enhancing what you teach.* Woodbridge: John Catt Educational Ltd.

Rosenshine, B. (2012) 'Principles of Instruction: Research-Based Strategies That All Teachers Should Know' in *American Educator*, 36(1), pp.12–19.

Sherrington, T. (2017) *The Learning Rainforest: Great Teaching in Real Classrooms.* Woodbridge: John Catt Educational Ltd.

van den Akker, J. (2003). 'Curriculum perspectives: An introduction' in van den Akker, J., Kuiper, W. and Hameyer, U. (eds), *Curriculum landscapes and trends.* Netherlands: Springer, pp.1–10.

Wiliam, D. (2018) *Creating the Schools Our Children Need: Why What We're Doing Now Won't Help Much (And What We Can Do Instead).* West Palms Beach, FL: Learning Sciences International.

Wiliam, D. and Leahy, S. (2015) *Embedding Formative Assessment: Practical Techniques for K-12 Classrooms.* West Palm Beach, FL: Learning Sciences International.

Willingham, D.T. (2006) 'How Knowledge Helps' in *American Educator*, Spring 2006 [online] Available at: www.aft.org/periodical/american-educator/spring-2006/how-knowledge-helps (Accessed 18 December 2025).

Willingham, D.T. (2015) *Raising Kids Who Read: What Parents and Teachers Can Do.* San Francisco, CA: Jossey-Bass.

Willingham, D.T. (2021) *Why Don't Students Like School? A Cognitive Scientist Answers Questions About How the Mind Works and What It Means for the Classroom.* San Francisco, CA: Jossey-Bass.

Young, M. (2020) 'From Powerful Knowledge to the Powers of Knowledge' in Sealy, C. (ed.) *The researchED Guide to The Curriculum.* Woodbridge: John Catt Educational Ltd, pp.19–30.

Young, M., Lambert, D., Roberts, C. and Roberts, M. (2014) *Knowledge and the Future School: Curriculum and Social Justice.* London: Bloomsbury Academic.

Acknowledgements

Power Up Your Curriculum is my sixth book. As with the previous five, I am extremely grateful for the support I have had from so many people in writing it. These include the publishing team at Hachette Learning, with particular thanks to Anders Ingram, Alex Duffy and Emilie Kerton; Carl Hendrick, who has written a brilliant foreword; Lindsay Paterson, for reading and offering comments on an advance copy of the manuscript; Daisy Christodoulou, Jim Heal, Mary Myatt, Robin Macpherson, Tom Bennett and Andrew Percival for writing such great testimonials; and finally to my husband, Jamie, for all of the support he continues to give me in the background.

Text Credits

The Publishers would like to thank the following for permission to reproduce copyright material.

pp.3 & 72 Two excerpts from *A Short History of Nearly Everything 2.0* by Bill Bryson. Copyright © Bill Bryson, 2003, 2025. Published by Transworld and reprinted by permission of Penguin Books Limited in the UK; Broadway Books, an imprint of Random House, a division of Penguin Random House LLC in the USA; and Anchor Canada/Doubleday Canada, a division of Penguin Random House Canada Limited in Canada. All rights reserved; **p.14** Excerpt from *Cleverlands: The Secrets Behind the Success of the World's Education Superpowers* by Lucy Creehan. Unbound, 2016. Reproduced by permission of Lucy Creehan; **p.48** Three definitions from *Oxford Dictionary Online* published by Oxford University Press (ELT). Reproduced with permission of the Licensor through PLSclear; **pp.60 & 76** Excerpts from *Curriculum for Excellence: Experiences and Outcomes*, Education Scotland (https://auth.education.gov.scot/media/wpsnskgv/all-experiencesoutcomes18.pdf). Contains public sector information licensed under the Open Government Licence v3.0. (https://www.nationalarchives.gov.uk/doc/open-government-licence/version/3/); **pp.84–5** Excerpt from *Meta-skills Progression Framework*, Skills Development Scotland. Reproduced by permission of Skills Development Scotland; **pp.102 & 104–6** From *Core Knowledge Sequence*, © Core Knowledge Foundation; used by permission of the Core Knowledge® Foundation, all rights reserved. Use of this Material does not constitute endorsement of the Work by the Core Knowledge Foundation.

Personalised professional development from Hachette Learning Academy

A simple way to boost career progression, staff motivation and educational excellence.

Our online courses are:

- Aligned with **teaching competency frameworks**
- **Written by experts in education**, including Hachette Learning authors (formerly John Catt)
- Created to enable educators to **develop core competencies** linked to their professional development aspirations
- **Powered by adaptive learning,** to accommodate a diverse range of skills, knowledge and understanding
- Designed to support **effective learning and high-impact teaching**

www.hachettelearning.com/academy

hachette LEARNING